Historical Criticism and Theological Interpretation of Scripture

Toward a Hermeneutics of Consent

Peter Stuhlmacher

Translated and with an Introduction by
Roy A. Harrisville

FORTRESS PRESS   Philadelphia

This book is a translation of the essay by Peter Stuhlmacher, "Historische Kritik und theologische Schriftauslegung" from the collection of essays by the same author, *Schriftauslegung auf dem Wege zur biblischen Theologie* (Göttingen: Vandenhoeck & Ruprecht, 1975).

Library of Congress Catalog Card Number 76–62606
ISBN 0–8006–1258–2

6175F77   Printed in the United States of America   1–1258

Historical Criticism
and
Theological Interpretation
of Scripture

Contents

Introduction
by Roy A. Harrisville

It may strike the reader as ironic that in a country such as Germany, in which the putting of historical questions is allegedly inhibited by systematic concerns, we should encounter in Peter Stuhlmacher a scholar who sounds an alarm respecting the autonomy, the independence, and the standoffishness assumed by the historical critic. But the irony is softened by the fact that the theological predicament in Germany has become twin sister to our own. Fifteen years ago it may have been possible for a continental scholar to suggest that American disinterest in the task of Bible interpretation reflected naïve confidence in historical method. Now, it is admitted, the chickens of the Enlightenment have come home to roost.

Once upon a time Friedrich Schleiermacher wrote in his *Brief Outline* that Christian theology is

> that assemblage of scientific knowledge and practical instruction without the possession and application of which a united leadership of the Christian church . . . is not possible. . . . When this same knowledge is acquired and possessed without relation to the government of the church, it ceases to be theological and devolves to those sciences to which it belongs according to its varied content.[1]

How, in what manner Schleiermacher conceived the union of the scientific pursuit of theology and the "government" of the church is not at issue, merely the fact that in the opinion of some, here and across the water, what once was joined together has been put asunder, has come unstuck, or, to return to Schleiermacher, the scientific study of theology has "devolved to those sciences to which it belongs according to its varied content."

1. Friedrich Schleiermacher, *Brief Outline on the Study of Theology,* trans. Terrence N. Tice (Richmond: John Knox Press, 1966), p. 20.

We shall leave it to Stuhlmacher to trace the route leading to this divorce. He does it clearly and by means of some embarrassing illustrations from the literature of our spiritual forbears. The *commencement* of that painful journey to diastasis he fixes in the penetration of historical research on the part of what is usually termed "Cartesian" thought. Descartes himself was not an enemy of the faith. Quite the contrary—his purpose was to observe certain "first principles" or causes of everything that is or might be in the world, and without paying that world any mind apart from the God who created it. But the "oath which he sware," never to accept as true anything he did not clearly know to be such, appeared to establish only the observer and his method—nothing more. For the "subject," everything had become an "object"—the world, mankind, God—and everything guaranteed its "objectivity" through the method. In short, the scientist had become detached, loosed from the "prejudice" of tradition or from some nonempirical, nondemonstrable vision or notion or idea he once called "truth." He learned to revel in the detachment, to call it "scientific," and he began to require that detachment of all engaged in scholarly enterprise. Whether or not that conception was first launched by Descartes, it soon made its home wherever two or three were gathered.

In 1636 Harvard was founded as a "conduit" for concepts from the Old World, a defender of the freedom of the "republic of letters," a "third force" coordinate with state and church, and some thirty years later altered its seal to read *Veritas,* just *Veritas.* In 1701 Yale was founded by the son of the designer of Harvard's first seal (*Christo et Ecclesiae*)—to offset the latter's "defection." But it needed only time till Mory's poor little lambs sang of portraying "all men and movements with equal detachment." As for the Presbyterians in New York, their school learned to live "by its brains," which being interpreted meant: "We are not now obliged to ask what Bible or creed or church requires, but what the facts teach, and we are able to move in the field of theology with the same freedom that the scientist enjoys in any other field."[2] Let

2. From the inaugural address of Arthur Cushman McGiffert at Union Theological Seminary, 1917, in Henry Sloane Coffin, *A Half Century of Union Theological Seminary 1896–1945* (New York: Charles Scribner's Sons, 1954), p. 105.

Veritas stand for the values and norms which science creates for itself once "truth" is no longer a given.

In historical theology it has often been the practice with us to distinguish the "descriptive" from the "hermeneutical" task, to keep separate what the text of the Bible "meant" when first uttered or written from what it "means," from its significance for the present. Such distinction we believed would compel the scholar to keep to whatever layers of meaning inhered in the text itself, without intruding whatever in him threatened to modernize his material. For some at least, this distinction would yield a view, a unity or theology normative for interpretation. But it is precisely this assumption which for Stuhlmacher has become specious, gratuitous. The expectation that the scholar was able in some fashion to hold himself aloof from the objects of his research and thus allow them to speak for themselves has lain unfulfilled. But if Stuhlmacher and those in our own bailiwick who have sounded alarm—Brevard Childs, Walter Wink, the structuralists; not at all look-alikes, but all with their mouth to the whistle—are correct, this vaunted "functionalism" (Stuhlmacher calls it *Strukturgesetzlichkeit*) in historical-criticism has resulted in a mammoth misinterpretation of scripture, since once faith was reckoned to be disadvantageous to the descriptive task, seven devils worse than the first assumed its place. The notion of "objectivity," according to which one may proceed without prior opinion to the objects of his research, belongs with Thomas Hardy's "native" to the trappings and souvenirs of a romantic past.

What then? Abandon science, abandon historical-critical method since, on the pretext of "objectivity," it has become prey to any master? Karl Barth once parried the suggestion that he was an enemy of historical-criticism with the retort that for him the historical-critical method needed to be more critical. What he meant may have had little to do with the discipline then or currently defined. Eberhard Busch reports Barth's conversation with Ernst Käsemann in 1960 in which Barth puckishly queried, "What does 'historical' mean? And 'critical'? And what is the significance of the hyphen between the two words?"[3] But if we

3. Eberhard Busch, *Karl Barth*, trans. John Bowden (Philadelphia: Fortress Press, 1976), p. 448.

abandon the historical-critical task the result is the same as if we undertake it under the assumption of objectivity—ideology, in this case the ideology of William Allen White's "man on a white horse":

> In general, the art of all truly great national leaders consists . . . first of all in refusing to divide a people's attention, and always in fixing upon a single opponent. . . . As soon as the wavering mass sees itself in conflict with too many enemies, objectivity will at once set in and prompt the question whether all the others are really wrong . . .? But with that comes the first crippling of one's own strength.

The paragraph is from Hitler's *Mein Kampf*,[4] but could just as well have been penned by others of recent memory on this side of the Atlantic.

Stuhlmacher does not shy away from a "catalogue of vices" in his own discipline, but he reserves his most critical comments for a former Tübingen student, Gerhard Maier, whose call to substitute for the scientific basis of biblical exegesis a "spiritual" and self-evident Bible exposition within the circle of the reborn has now received the imprimatur of an American denomination for which the six-day creation, an historical Adam, and a literal interpretation of the Book of Jonah are a datum of faith. It is one thing to decry science's divorce from some all-embracing truth. It is quite another to damn it on principle.

We are between the tree and the bark. If we undertake critical research of the Bible, or if we abandon that research, the result appears to be the same. To paraphrase an old saw of Luther: "Whoever does theology, sometimes comes a-cropper; whoever doesn't, comes a-cropper anyhow." Stuhlmacher, however, is not ready to agree that the historical-critical method has proved fruitless. For him the dilemma or divorce does not derive from some inherent fault in the tool, as though it were an instrument of the devil's own devising, or were hell-bent on fixing single, "univocal" meanings to every blessed verse of Holy Writ. Stuhlmacher is rather convinced that, aside from the interior witness of the Spirit, the life of the Reformation churches is contingent upon their success with historical exegesis—a conviction which Roman Cath-

4. Adolf Hitler, *Mein Kampf* (Munich: Zentralverlag der NSDAP, 1944), p. 129.

olic scholars, with a notable exception or two, have come to share. But in light of the inability of such towering figures as Schlatter, Barth, and Bultmann to achieve any synthesis between the historical and the theological, what is to be done? Agreed, historical method compels the Christian community to acknowledge the sovereignty of that God who makes his redemptive activity contingent upon an historical particular, an acknowledgement without which the Gospels could scarcely have been written. But also agreed, the pretext of "detachment" under which the vast array of scholars attempts to give precision to that contingency has loosed biblical interpretation from its moorings. Laying claim to the title of "reputable historian" has led us to a kind of kerygmatic autophagism, to faith's feeding upon itself, its historical occasions reduced to the mathematical point of a "that"—"that" Jesus lived and died. Or, it has led to a kind of *heilsgeschichtlich* cannibalism, to a normalizing of the historical rendered transparent to research—the requirement of faith reduced to a mere "echo."

In a handful of steps, Stuhlmacher offers his solution to the dilemma under the rubric "Hermeneutics of Consent." Acknowledging the indispensability as well as the limits of the historical method, he appeals for its "expansion" in an "effective-historical consciousness." Stuhlmacher thus adds to the principles of criticism, analogy, and correlation once enunciated by Ernst Troeltsch a fourth principle designed to yield that consciousness of effects but without robbing the historian of the necessity for critically examining his texts. Stuhlmacher calls it the principle of "hearing," from which will result a dialogue between interpreter and text. In other words, Stuhlmacher urges the historical critic to operate with a view of history and reality which is open to "transcendence." Now a scholar who contends that the critical and theological concerns of scripture interpretation may still be wedded cannot require less, once he has exposed the notion of "objectivity" as myth, but for all that still defines the critical enterprise as driving to the heart of the matter.

Stuhlmacher does not assume that only a believer can be an historian, but in the great market of options and biases available to the researcher, one, or perhaps several of which he is destined, fated to choose (unless, of course, he assays to slingshot himself out of historical existence), Stuhlmacher merely asks: "Why shall not the critic be obliged to "hear" the claim of transcendence which constitutes the very matter of the text? Nor does our author assume that once the text is heard the historian will have become a believer. No method can establish recognition of the biblical proclamation. What then might it mean for, say, a Franz Overbeck or the author of *The Passover Plot* to engage in criti cism within such a framework? For Stuhlmacher, it would mean to adopt the posture of *intellectus quaerens fidem*—understanding seeking faith.

This is certainly a modest requirement in light of the massive idealistic-romantic exactions made of the researcher in the years behind us, a modest assumption. And there is something in the American tradition of thought which ought to rise to Stuhlmacher's bait: "If we believe that no bell in us tolls to let us know for certain when truth is in our grasp, then it seems a piece of idle fantasticality to preach so solemnly our duty of waiting for the bell."[5]

Perhaps Stuhlmacher's most signal contribution in this volume, and the point at which a genuine synthesis between the historical and theological begins clearly to emerge, is his contention that the "consent" of the investigator, his readiness to "hear" the claim of transcendence raised by his text, must be given definition by that community which has ventured its existence upon it. In addition to its theological validity, this argument expresses a truth of logic so commonplace and homespun as to be easily overlooked—the truth that knowledge is rooted in the "social principle." In the *Popular Science Monthly* for 1877, an obscure assistant in the United States Coast Survey, who is now the acknowledged father of American pragmatism, illustrated the absurdity of isolated, private reasoning:

> If a man had to choose between drawing a card from a pack containing twenty-five red cards and a black one, or from a pack containing twenty-five black cards and a red one, and if the drawing of a red card were destined to transport him to eternal felicity, and that of a black one to consign him to everlasting woe,

5. William James, "The Will to Believe," *Essays On Faith And Morals* (New York: World Publishing Co. 1962), p. 61.

it would be folly to deny that he ought to prefer the pack containing the larger proportion of red cards. . . . But suppose he should choose the red pack, and should draw the wrong card, what consolation would he have? He might say that he had acted in accordance with reason, but that would only show that his reason was absolutely worthless. And if he should choose the right card, how could he regard it as anything but a happy accident?

If Charles Sanders Peirce's cardplayer were not merely concerned with his own fate, or did not draw from the red pack out of mere habit, but had a care for what might happen to every other person in the same embarrassment, he would draw from the red pack and at least prove himself a logician. "There can be no sense in reasoning in an isolated case," concluded Peirce, since to be logical "men should not be selfish."[6]

Stuhlmacher, former pupil and assistant of Ernst Käsemann, does not leave the reader in doubt regarding his theological antecedents. He is quick to assert that his attempt at solution of the dilemma of historical criticism is fraught with some subjectivity, and classifies himself as moving along the boundaries between kerygmatic theology, Pietism, and "biblically-oriented Lutheranism." And though highly critical of current solutions to the dilemma, he flatly admits that the attempts of Eberhard Jüngel, Friedrich Mildenberger, and Wolfhart Pannenberg to wed the historical and theological concerns have furnished him a bearing for his own.

The point at which the reader may require assistance is that of Stuhlmacher's interest in the investigations of Hans Georg Gadamer, Bultmann's star pupil in the field of philosophy. The degree of Stuhlmacher's use of Gadamer's *Truth and Method*,[7] is sufficient to make of this volume a text or primer on the uses of contemporary thought as vehicle for New Testament exposition. Here are a few instances at which the lines in Stuhlmacher and Gadamer converge:

Stuhlmacher's criticism of the autonomy of the historical method is reminiscent of Gadamer's exposure of the naïvete of the historian who assumes he can abandon his own concepts and

6. Charles S. Peirce, "The Doctrine of Chances," *Essays In The Philosophy of Science* (New York: Bobbs-Merrill Co., 1957), pp. 64–67.
7. Hans Georg Gadamer, *Truth and Method*, translation edited by Garrett Barden and John Cumming (New York: Seabury Press, 1975).

think only in those of the epoch to be researched—only to fall prey to biases he has left unexamined.[8]

Our author's introduction of his "fourth principle," that of "hearing," occurs at precisely the point at which Gadamer summons his readers to a critical hermeneutic—at the point of the Enlightenment's discrediting of all "prejudice."[9]

The definition which Stuhlmacher gives to the "effective-historical consciousness" must have had Gadamer for its author.

The refusal to model the humane after the natural sciences, or to reduce the task of interpretation to the intention of the author; the assumption that time is not an abyss which must be bridged but that understanding is borne by the historical movement within which life itself is lived, and that for this reason sheer facts cannot be the real object of research but rather the significance of events within the totality of historical self-awareness; the description of "hermeneutical consciousness" as dealing with the tradition through which the heart of the matter comes to its expression; the designation of "openness" to tradition as the highest mode of such consciousness; and the suggestion that the "effective-historical consciousness" may not be new, but certainly new as applied to method—in it all Gadamer appears to have paved the way.[10]

Even Stuhlmacher's commitment to *sola scriptura* has its counterpart in Gadamer's insistence upon the interpreter's submission to the text's claim to dominate the mind. His description of the dialogue between interpreter and text within the context of the church's experience has support in Gadamer's description of the raising of what is transmitted in literary form to the contemporaneity of conversation, in his discussion of the "fusion of horizons," and of the impossibility of separating scientific knowledge from edifying application.[11]

Finally, respecting Stuhlmacher's contention that only those who venture to live by faith may understand, one sentence from Gadamer suffices to indicate that both have at least drawn from

8. Ibid., pp. 357–58.
9. Ibid., p. 244.
10. Ibid., pp. 7–8, 23–24, 250, 253, 262, 264, 267, 303, 321, 324, 336, 338.
11. Ibid., pp. 273, 276, 278, 292–93, 296–97, 332.

the same well: "Modern hermeneutics, as a Protestant discipline
... assumes that the word of scripture addresses us and that only
the person who allows himself to be addressed—whether he believes or whether he doubts—understands. Hence the primary
thing is application."[12]

This little book, then, with the exception of a brief essay published in 1968,[13] will introduce the English-reading audience to a
man little known outside his own country, except to members of
the "guild," but who has already distinguished himself through
the publication of two major Pauline studies.[14] And, since Stuhlmacher is as quick to acknowledge his debt to Gadamer as to his
theological teachers, here—if not for the first time, at any rate
here—English-speaking students of theology have an opportunity
to consider whether and how well one current and thoughtful
understanding of the New Testament corresponds with one significant, contemporary perception of truth—a perception not without its counterparts in our own American heritage of thought.

Now the reader must decide whether or not it is time for
biblical research to leave off apotheosizing "the bare conceiving
faculty"; time to admit that "the mind functions for the sake of
ends which do not exist in the impressions we receive from our
senses"; time to risk "consent," to venture the hypothesis of transcendence; and time to be logical, not selfish. With such a risk,
Stuhlmacher believes, science is not robbed but rather established
—it is merely ideology which has gone out with the bath water.

12. Ibid., pp. 296–97.
13. Peter Stuhlmacher, "Behold, I make all things new!" *Lutheran World*
15, (1968): 3–15.
14. Peter Stuhlmacher, *Gerechtigkeit Gottes bei Paulus* (Göttingen: Vandenhoeck & Ruprecht, 1966); and *Das paulinische Evangelium, 1. Vorge-
schichte* (Göttingen: Vandenhoeck & Ruprecht, 1968).

Author's Preface

This volume is not my first attempt at coming to terms with the dilemma of historical criticism. Rather, it contains reflections on the theme which were presented for discussion in the *Zeitschrift für Theologie und Kirche* 68 (1971): 121–61, and in the *Zeitschrift für neutestamentliche Wissenschaft* 63 (1972): 18–26. Similar reflections were also submitted for discussion in the preparatory studies for the *Evangelisch-Katholischer Kommentar zum Neuen Testament Heft* 4 (1972): 1–55, and under the title "Zur Methoden- und Sachproblematik einer interkonfessionellen Auslegung des Neuen Testaments." Due to the subject matter treated in those studies and in this volume, the reader acquainted with the scholarly literature will note a certain resemblance and even overlapping. However, the studies earlier submitted were largely thetical in nature, and were not set within the larger context of the history of biblical interpretation. It is the purpose of this volume to furnish just such a context, as well as to give my hermeneutical reflections their needed precision. The book thus gathers up and gives specificity to earlier discussions of the hermeneutical problem.

Abbreviations

BhTh	Beiträge zur historischen Theologie
CH	Church History
DtPfBl	Deutsches Pfarrerblatt
Ev Komm	Evangelische Kommentare
FRLANT	Forschungen zur Religion und Literatur des Alten und Neuen Testaments
KuD	Kerygma und Dogma
SVG	Sammlung Gemeinverständlicher Vorträge und Schriften aus dem Gebiet der Theologie und Religionsgeschichte
ThB	Theologische Bücherei
ThQ	Theologische Quartalschrift
ThSt	Theological Studies
WUNT	Wissenschaftliche Untersuchungen zum Neuen Testament
ZNW	Zeitschrift für die neutestamentliche Wissenschaft und die Kunde der älteren Kirche
ZSTh	Zeitschrift für systematische Theologie
ZThK	Zeitschrift für Theologie und Kirche

Introduction: The Problem of Historical Criticism

In his 1950 programmatic essay on "The Significance of the Critical Historical Method for Church and Theology in Protestantism," Gerhard Ebeling made the following statement: "The question of the critical historical method is far from being a formal, technical problem of methodology: it is a question which, from the historical and factual point of view, touches on the deepest foundations and the most difficult interconnections of theological thinking and of the church situation."[1] This statement is no less valid today, though, or precisely because, twenty-five years of theological study have transpired since Ebeling's study. We can see this most easily when we note briefly the contemporary situation regarding the phenomenon and problem of historical criticism.

Today, after long and painful struggle, the historical-critical method is not only recognized within Catholicism as an exegetical tool, but is actually commended to Catholic exegetes in official ecclesiastical pronouncements. Under these conditions Catholic exegesis is advancing freed and heartened toward an as yet unknown range and level which sets much Protestant work in the shade. In contrast, Protestant theology finds no peace at all in its historical-critical study, to say nothing of experiencing a like upsurge. With or without his consent, the Protestant exegete who labors in historical-critical fashion today sees himself involved in a war on many fronts, marked by the following salients:

THE THREE FRONTS

Though Protestant theology has long recognized the historical-critical method and practices it with noteworthy success, and

1. Gerhard Ebeling, *Word and Faith*, trans. James W. Leitch (Philadelphia: Fortress Press, 1963), p. 22.

though for its historical disciplines any scientific alternative to this method is out of the question, Fundamentalism and Pietism are still filled with a measure of profound mistrust in historical criticism. After the alleged shipwreck of historical-critical method they are summoning us back to a reformational-spiritual, or even biblicistic and uncritical exposition of scripture.[2]

Today this obviously serious but (viewed from the history of theology) actually nonreflective call to repentance is not countered simply by the so-called radical Bible criticism which eventually took on confessional character, but also by that circle of Protestants which sees at work in the biblical sciences an inadmissible domestication of a method originally emancipative and critical of authority. In place of such restriction this circle advocates and effects a transfer of the once radical historical criticism to a socio-critical political hermeneutic.

The third front moves between these two extremes and strives for a considered, self-critical adaptation of historical criticism to the scientific and theological needs and possibilities of the present, however viewed and judged. When we consider that this third front is held and defended by such diverse groups as "theological pietism," as Ernst Käsemann once called it,[3] intent through its historical study on concretizing the gospel and in a measure actually defending it; by that circle of Bultmann's pupils loyal to the church and denounced by Dorothee Soelle as "kerygmatic neoorthodoxy";[4] by Lutherans occupied with *Heilsgeschichte*; by Reformed theologians concerned for solid historical

2. See, e.g., Hellmuth Frey, "Um den Ansatz theologischer Arbeit," *Abraham unser Vater. Juden und Christen im Gespräch über die Bibel*. Festschrift für Otto Michel zum 60. Geburtstag, ed. Otto Betz, Martin Hengel, and Peter Schmidt (Leiden: E. J. Brill, 1963), pp. 153–180, and "Ernst Käsemann—Überwinder oder Gefangener des Existentialismus und Historismus?" *Das Kreuz Jesu und die Krise der Evangelischen Kirche*, ed. Sven Findeisen, Hellmuth Frey, and Wilhelm Johanning (Bad Liebenzell: Verlag der Liebenzeller Mission, 1967), pp. 94–124; Gerhard Bergmann, *Alarm um die Bibel*, 5te Auflage (Gladbeck: Schriftenmissions-Verlag, 1974); Gerhard Bergmann and Hermann Diem, *Das gleiche Evangelium* (Düsseldorf: Verlag Presseverband der Evangelischen Kirche im Rheinland, 1967), pp. 7ff., 48ff.; Gerhard Maier, *The End of the Historical-Critical Method*, trans. Edwin W. Leveranz and Rudolf F. Norden (St. Louis: Concordia Publishing House, 1977). On this latter volume, see the excursus on pp. 66–70.

3. Ernst Käsemann, *New Testament Questions of Today*, trans. W. J. Montague (Philadelphia: Fortress Press, 1969), p. 3.

4. Dorothee Soelle, *Political Theology, trans.* John Shelley (Philadelphia: Fortress Press, 1974), pp. 19, 22, 38, 77.

and theological study, as well as by many others, then the perplexing situation in which we Protestants find ourselves becomes fairly clear, since the last named groups do not at all agree but make common cause only through being jointly attacked from the right and the left.

Contemporary Protestant theology is thus still hounded and harried by the fundamental problems of historical criticism. In addition, just now the relevance of the entire historical-critical formulation of the question is in part subject to serious doubt in theological and ecclesiastical circles. For this reason some Protestants and Catholics believe they must turn from the exegetical-historical to contemporary, empirical, service-oriented, and political approaches to the question.

THE NEED FOR CLARIFICATION

For the sake of his special task and the indissoluble connection between the church and the biblical canon, an exegete cannot share this retreat from the historical-critical dilemma. Rather, he must always be aware of his own scientific and theological possibilities. This also applies to all theologically trained Christians who regard the exposition of Holy Scripture, that is, a scientifically responsible exposition, as indispensable to the church.

Accordingly, I will attempt in what follows to clarify the possibilities and limits of historical-critical exegesis within the framework of Protestant theology today. I undertake this clarification as exegete and New Testament scholar, conscious that a church historian or dogmatician, given the circumstances, could set the accents elsewhere. I am also aware that a goodly amount of subjectivity marks my attempt because I must classify myself as moving along the boundaries between kerygmatic theology, Pietism, and biblically-oriented Lutheranism, and thus in that middle salient sketched above.

Scripture Interpretation in the Past

If we intend to achieve clarity regarding the basic questions at issue in historical criticism today, it is absolutely necessary first to visualize the development, legacy, and basic problems of scripture exposition in the church. This is advisable because a considerable percentage of the questions which appear insoluble today derives from our being burdened with the failures and oversimplifications of earlier generations. We can sooner urge the revision of untenable positions as we reflect again on those partly long-forgotten simplifications. But calling to mind basic problems of exposition in the church is also important because it allows us to see how few hermeneutical positions are set simply by individual whim. Rather, they represent life-decisions in which the irreplaceable and independent achievement of single historical personalities is bound up with historical enterprises and sanctions.

Keeping only to strategic junctures in Christian scripture exposition, at least six stages must be marked within the scope of our reflections, and their basic features sketched.

BEGINNINGS

It is worth noting that Christian scripture interpretation is not first an effort and achievement of the ancient church. As early as in the New Testament it accompanies and in essence determines the origin, formulation, and unfolding of the gospel of Jesus as the Christ of God.

In the well-known antitheses of the Sermon on the Mount (Matt: 5.21–48), and in his work of reconciliation attended by signs, Jesus himself encounters us as Messianic interpreter and fulfiller of the Mosaic law and the reconciling will of Yahweh.

In his contingent spiritual authority Jesus harks back to the tradition and text of the Old Testament to interpret, enunciate, and complete its witness to God by his appearance. In the same measure as Jesus' appearance and behavior were violently disputed in his lifetime, he unfailingly leads his disciples into a process of critical scripture exposition. Despite decisive modifications, this process has not ceased to this day and may not be interrupted as long as the churches are oriented to scripture so as to preserve their identity.

At the beginning of this critical exposition, which at first was applied only to the Old Testament literature, the weightiest perceptions and decisions already emerge. If in his Messianic conduct Jesus appeared to the Jewish Sanhedrists who sentenced him and handed him over to Pilate as a despiser of the law and a blaspheming Antimessiah,[1] the Easter events taught Jesus' followers to confess him as Son of God and Messianic Reconciler, and at the direction of that same Old Testament which Jesus' opponents supposed had been dishonored by the Son of Man.

We can best track this dispute over the proper understanding of the Old Testament—a dispute as old as the gospel itself—from that point where the oldest sermon-outlines and credal formulas speak the language of the Old Testament and refer to the scripture's fulfillment in Jesus' death and his being raised. 1 Corinthians 15:3-5 reads that Christ (that is, Jesus as true Messiah) died for our sins and was raised on the third day "in accordance with the scriptures (of the Old Testament)." Luke 24:27,32 indicates in legendary but historically appropriate fashion how the risen Christ opens the eyes of his own to the christological dimension of the Old Testament scriptures. Finally, the oldest speeches in Acts make clear to what extent the beginnings of Christian gospel proclamation among the Jews were stamped by scriptural arguments for Jesus' Messiahship, the saving meaning of his mission, and his being raised.

A few years after these missionary beginnings Paul proclaims and in disputation unfolds his gospel of justification as an exegete of the Old Testament, that is, as a scribe of the Pharisees who

1. On the term "Antimessiah," see Martin Hengel, "Gewalt und Gewaltlosigkeit," *CH* 118 (1971): 44.

has been won to the faith by the risen Christ. He now places in the service of his eschatological Lord a talent for systematic scripture exposition (according to the prevailing standard) gleaned while a Jew in Jerusalem. Paul achieves an exegetical victory over the Jewish polemic that according to Deuteronomy 21:23 Jesus died on the cross as a blasphemer signally cursed by God. The apostle takes up this Jewish charge in Galatians 3:13 and parries it by showing that Jesus died the accursed death on the cross in our stead, in order at God's behest to remove from sinners the curse of the law. It was thus not Jesus who by his alleged blasphemous activity shipwrecked on the curse of God by virtue of the law. Quite the contrary—the Mosaic law, damning the sinner in its deadly power, shipwrecked on the sacrifice of Jesus, the Righteous One, and this by virtue of the will of God! Through such an exegetically-based proclamation of Jesus Christ as the end of the law (Romans 10:4), Paul definitively opens the way to the primitive Christian mission to the Gentiles.

With his pioneering distinction between scripture and letter (*graphē* and *gramma*) or Spirit and letter (2 Corinthians 3), that is, between the Old Testament viewed from faith as a life-creating word of God and from Jewish unbelief as a killing law, he once for all bequeathes to Christian hermeneutics categories and criteria without which a Christian exegesis hereafter can no longer be carried on.[2] Paul's procedure finds substantial continuation in the skillful exegesis of Hebrews and in the terse formulation of the Johannine prologue: "The law was given through Moses; grace and truth came through Jesus Christ" (John 1:17).

Thus, New Testament proclamation already assumes a critical exposition of the Old Testament tradition. This critical exposition, initiated by Jesus and, after Easter, in its essence christological, actually exhibits an essential feature of the gospel. Not only in Christian theology, but in the exegesis of the New Testament itself, all the current possibilities of a rational exegetical method are set in the service of faith. New Testament scripture interpretation thus lives by the empowering of the Holy Spirit,

2. See Otto Michel, *Paulus und seine Bibel* (Gütersloh: C. Bertelsmann, 1972), pp. 173ff.; Ernst Käsemann, "The Spirit and the Letter," *Perspectives on Paul*, trans. Margaret Kohl (Philadelphia: Fortress Press, 1971), pp. 138–66.

that is, by the presence of the risen Christ, and draws a hermeneutical distinction between Spirit and letter (scripture and letter), between a word of scripture willfully misunderstood and a word of scripture which discloses itself to faith and instructs it.

ANCIENT AND MEDIEVAL EXPOSITION

When we turn to scripture interpretation in the ancient church and the Middle Ages, we note first a decisive modification over against the New Testament era. Exegesis is now applied to a churchly canon composed of Old and New Testaments, and in a real sense becomes an ecclesiastical interpretation of Holy Scripture.

The Canon

Various motives underly the efforts to construct a comprehensive biblical canon. These efforts originate in the second century A.D., and conclude for a time at the end of the fourth or beginning of the fifth century with Athanasius' thirty-ninth Easter epistle of 376 and the February 20, 405 letter of Pope Innocent I to the Bishop of Toulouse.

As for the literature of the Old Testament, valued beyond dispute by Christians as Holy Scripture until well into the second century, congregations of the ancient church are shaken by the fact that from the end of the first century Judaism takes thought for its own canon, creates translations to rival the Septuagint received by the Christians, and conclusively breaks with the Christian communities. To this are added Marcion's and Christian Gnosticism's rejection of the Old Testament content and liturgy and its alleged inferior God of vengeance. Both Jewish practice and the so-called heretical movements in their own ranks give the orthodox communities occasion to insist on "their" Old Testament and to take thought for its continuance.

At the same time, the following circumstances compel these communities to undertake a canonical selection from out of the primitive Christian literature already in use and read at worship. The more or less rank growth of allegedly apostolic literature requires a distinction between authentic and secondary material, in order to support one's own doctrine and position by aid of the authentic tradition. Marcion's and the Gnostics' one-sided expropriation of Paul leads to ranking the extra-Pauline epistolary and narrative material with the Pauline letters. Reaction to the ascetic and apocalyptic enthusiasm of Montanus and his disciples who soon form their own clique breeds reserve toward Christian apocalypses in wide circulation, and toward early Christian writings which appear to further the ethical rigorism of the Montanists. In all, there arises a process of concentration and collection by which the chief writings of the New Testament, that is, the Synoptics, the Pauline letters, and Acts (included at some remove due to content), followed hard by the occasionally disputed Gospel of John, soon constituted the kernel of the New Testament. For a longer period only Hebrews, the Revelation of John, and a small portion of the Catholic Epistles were disputed. As for the Old Testament, in the time of Athanasius and Innocent I it was still not made clear to what extent the Wisdom of Solomon and the book of Jesus Sirach, Esther, Judith, and Tobit—thus a portion of the Septuagint apocrypha—should be added to the canon or merely used in the instruction of catechumens.

When we inquire into the theological components in this formation of a comprehensive canon we ought first to note that in the church Old and New Testament, despite the uncontested hermeneutical primacy of the latter, are always seen together. Thus, strictly speaking, a Christian problematic of the Old and New Testament, each isolated from the other, simply does not exist. From the outset Christian faith puts the question—which engages us to this moment—as to *how* the two Testaments belong together.

Second, we must note that bishops and metropolitans, the real court of arbitration in the church, applied the criterion of apostolicity to the primitive and early Christian literature eligible for selection. The criterion was very elastic, since it aided simultaneous inquiry into the age, origin, and material agreement of a writing with the symbol—traced to the apostles respecting its content—or *regula fidei* (in Greek: *kanōn tēs pisteos*). Because this rule of faith in turn was understood as a compendium of the faith proclaimed and taught in the New Testament writings, from the very beginning an indissoluble reciprocal relationship existed between the New Testament canon and the church's confession of faith, a relationship which forbids our regarding the canon as merely a creation of the church. If it is true that the church gave birth to the canon as selection, it is also true that by establishing this selection the church already stood under the unquestioned claim, above all, of the chief New Testament writings and the Old Testament promise.

Finally, when we look for that systematic view of the whole which makes possible a comprehensive biblical canon, we need to note that it can most clearly be seen in Justin Martyr (ca. 110–65), namely, in the shape of his Logos-doctrine.[3] Christ is witnessed to as Logos by the Old Testament and by the apostolic literature, of which Justin gives the Gospels special value. In both Christ is witnessed to as the Logos insofar as the Holy Spirit, inspiring Old and New Testament authors, is not separable from the Christ-Logos, but one of his most important modes of appearance. The Logos-Christology together with the doctrine of inspiration thus embraces the Old and New Testament canon at its very inception, indeed as a constitutive bond. Spirit and letter belong together, and the old Pauline distinction is now promoted to the key hermeneutical theory of exegesis in the church.

Allegorical Exegesis

The ecclesiastical interpretation of scripture which was to draw on this canon of Old and New Testament and lift from it the biblical witness to truth in service to the church now required a method which would penetrate to this spiritual witness and at the same time effectually bind the biblical literature with the community's faith. This method lay ready to hand in the shape of the theory of the multiple or, better, multi-dimensional sense of scripture and the so-called allegorical exposition yielding this

3. For this insight I am indebted to a lecture delivered by Martin Elze at Sindlingen Castle, February 24, 1974, before the editorial council of *ZThK* on the theme, "Die Entstehung und Relevanz der Schrift als Kanon." On the topic, see Eric Francis Osborn, "Justin Martyr," *BhTh* 47 (1973): 28ff., 87ff.; and Elze, "Häresie und Einheit der Kirche im 2. Jahrhundert," *ZThK* 71 (1974): 404–5.

sense. Allegorical interpretation was shaped since the third
century B.C. in the centers of Hellenistic learning, Alexandria and
Pergamum. It was tested chiefly in the exegesis of the Homeric
writings, held to be inspired, and, interestingly enough, in conjunction with a strictly philological concern for establishing a
pure text of Homer's writings which to a degree were consider-
ably corrupted and often interpolated.

The chief goal of allegory is to extract the profound spiritual
sense hidden in the wording of a literary production inspired by
the Logos, and to lay it open to man's understanding. Hellenistic
Judaism, just as Judaism in the Palestinian motherland, set out
from the inspiration of its Holy Scriptures, and, as the example
of Philo of Alexandria indicates, made expert use of the allegorical method. From that point, the allegorization of texts makes its
way to the New Testament, as shown by Galatians 4:21–31 and
for example, Hebrews 3:6. It is not surprising, therefore, that
allegory was at once taken up in the church and to a degree
actually gained the mastery.

When we reflect on the idea of the Logos leading to the biblical canon we must admit that in such a christological-pneumatic
framework allegory offered an ideal method for exegesis. If it
was true of the Stoic that "he is entitled to interpret who is aware
of the Logos at work in him, the same Logos who spoke in the
hidden sayings of Homer," then in the "Christian sense he is
called to interpret whom the Holy Spirit has touched, and thus
can explain the scripture *pneumatikōs* in a way harmonious with
the Spirit." Participation in the Logos or Pneuma was regarded
by ancient exegetes, Christians or no, as the "pre-condition and
starting point of every interpretation." More, "Every exegesis
depends on following the Logos or Pneuma as norm. Through
the Logos, through the Pneuma, exegesis is given its method; the
method cannot be altered at will. Since there is only one Logos,
one Pneuma, which remains identical with itself and never errs,
the starting point, the way, and the goal are unequivocally
determined."[4]

Among early Christian expositors it was Origen above all (ca.

4. Heinrich Dörrie, "Zur Methodik antiker Exegese," ZNW 65 (1974):
135–36.

185–254) who in the best ancient philological and hermeneutical tradition gave the church confidence in its then current scientific and spiritual exposition, and through his famous Hexapla put us forever in his debt for the form of the Septuagint text.

Tertullian and the Rule of Faith

The comprehensive interpretative system in ancient and medieval exposition was finally fitted together by Tertullian. In a countermove against the disjunctive and in his opinion arbitrary interpretation of the Christian-Gnostic schools, Tertullian maintained that he alone is authorized for true exposition who belongs to the true, orthodox church, and that belief in the rule of faith cherished by this church—the aforementioned *regula fidei*—constitutes the sole true support in face of a host of possible individual interpretations. More, for Tertullian, cherishing and sharing this rule of faith is of overriding importance, indeed downright essential in face of the hazardous possibilities and pursuits of scientific scripture exegesis. Thus, with Tertullian, the living and teaching church together with the rule of faith it bears comes to stand above the interpretation of scripture. Tertullian himself claims and uses such exposition merely as a tool necessary to the church and entrusted to scholars for finding the truth. His *De praescriptione haereticorum* of ca. A.D. 203 reads:

> Provided the essence of the Rule is not disturbed, you may seek and discuss as much as you like. You may give full rein to your itching curiosity where any point seems unsettled and ambiguous or dark and obscure. There must surely be some brother endowed with the gift of knowledge who can teach you, someone who moves among the learned who will share your curiosity and your inquiry. In the last resort, however, it is better for you to remain ignorant, for fear that you come to know what you should not know. For you do know what you should know. "Thy faith hath saved thee," it says; not thy biblical learning. Faith is established in the Rule. There it has its law, and it wins salvation by keeping the law. Learning derives from curiosity and wins glory only from its zealous pursuit of scholarship. Let curiosity give place to faith, and glory to salvation. Let them at least be no hindrance, or let them keep quiet. To know nothing against the Rule is to know everything.[5]

5. Tertullian, "The Prescription Against The Heretics," trans. Stanley Lawrence Greenslade, in *The Library of Christian Classics*, 26 vols. (Philadelphia: Westminster Press, 1956), 5: 40. On the contemporary significance

With Tertullian's theses, with the allegorical interpretation of scripture established by Origen, and with the church's formation of a canon from the Old and New Testaments, we have before us the scaffold of ancient church exposition best suited to the late-ancient and medieval perception of truth. By penetrating to the unalterable, spiritual truth of faith in and behind the biblical texts, scripture interpretation gains a share in God's eternal truth revealed historically in the church and in its sacramental authority. Thus, true exposition can only be an exegesis which in faith serves the church's consciousness of faith.

Augustine and the Knowledge of God

This ecclesiastical system of interpretation is restated and impressed on the Middle Ages by Augustine (A.D. 354–430) in his famous treatise, De doctrina christiana, the most influential text on exposition in the church. For Augustine too, it is obvious that the goal of all interpretation and its normative framework is the church's rule of faith. Holy Scripture is correctly interpreted when the expositor is filled with love for God and his neighbor, and is willing to interpret the scripture in view of faith, hope, and love.

For Augustine the true task of interpretation requires first of all carefully revised texts and a clear concept of the compass and content of the inspired Old and New Testament canon, next, the knowledge of the original biblical languages, Hebrew and Greek, and finally the capacity appropriately to distinguish between the literal and derived sense of scripture. The rule for making this distinction is as follows: "Whatever there is in the word of God that cannot, when taken literally, be referred either to purity of life or soundness of doctrine, you may set down as figurative. Purity of life has reference to the love of God and one's neighbor; soundness of doctrine to the knowledge of God and one's neighbor."[6] The goal of the entire process of exposition is the knowl-

---

of Tertullian's hermeneutics see Otto Kuss, "Zur Hermeneutik Tertullians," Schriftauslegung, Beiträge zur Hermeneutik des Neuen Testaments und im Neuen Testament, ed. Josef Ernst (Munich: Ferdinand Schöningh, 1972), pp. 55–87.
6. A Select Library of the Nicene and Post-Nicene Fathers of the Christian Church, ed. Philip Schaff (Buffalo: Christian Literature Publishing Co., 1887), 2: 560–61.

edge of the love of Christ which forsakes all the pride of science, a love in which Christ is one with the Father, in order by this very love to experience the ground of all true existence.

Hence for Augustine and all who follow him, interpretation of Holy Scripture represents a process of spiritual knowledge, thought through in philological-systematic fashion. Led by the biblical word, the interpreter ascends in knowledge to God and, insofar as he opens himself to love, arrives at the divine ground of existence, in which the church has a miraculous share by virtue of its sacramental authority.

The Integration of Knowledge and Faith

In the churches of the East as well as the West, allegory finally came to rest and ossified in the commentaries of scholastic tradition, the catenae, glossa ordinaria, etc. In order to give new, unrestricted hearing to the scriptural word within and over against the church, a new beginning and a method of interpretation were required, which not only enabled one to suit texts and their wording to a churchly system of knowledge and faith, but also to allow them their own historical weight.

Before we look to Humanism and the Reformation, which attempted and achieved this new hermeneutical beginning, we must again briefly note the productivity of the ancient and medieval system of exposition. Within the framework of the then universal perception of truth, this exposition achieved an integration of scriptural utterance with the church's consciousness of faith, of spiritual life with scientific knowledge, and in this fashion long assisted the church toward a binding and evident proclamation of faith, to the extent that it then was possible. Within the framework of the interpretative system just sketched, the believing and teaching church finally took on too great weight. But this capacity for integration in ancient and medieval exegesis serves as guide, and subsequent Christian exposition cannot neglect the centuries' old experience that scripture truly discloses itself only to those who dare to exist by common faith in Christ as Christ's community, and as such hearken to the word of scripture. The symbol of this hermeneutical experience is still the doctrine of inspiration and the Logos.

REFORMATION EXPOSITION

When we set out from this background it seems quite remarkable that the Reformers do not intend, say, to abrogate the traditional system of interpretation, but merely to improve upon it! For Reformation exegesis as well, the Third Article of the Apostles' Creed is the decisive framework for all hermeneutical effort, and it is not at all about to abandon the teaching tradition of the church. Rather, it keeps expressly to the great symbols of the ancient church together with the doctrine of the Trinity as the dogmatically normative and valid insights of the church. In the Reformation, the hermeneutical circle encompassing scripture and the church's consciousness of faith is thus preserved intact. But what is decidedly new is the distribution of weight within this circle and thus the theological evaluation of the process of interpretation itself.

The Primacy of Scripture

Within that interpretative circle of scripture and church, Reformation exegesis no longer gives decisive weight to the teaching church, equipped with sacramental authority, but to the scripture. The church is also warned that it is in constant peril of shattering on itself and the weight of its tradition, and thus while on earth is always in need of reform and is only on the way to spiritual consummation. Scripture receives the accent in the hermeneutical circle because from it alone can be heard the gospel which decides life and death—the redeeming gospel of the mission, death, and raising of Christ for the salvation of the world. If it was stated earlier that scripture must be interpreted in the spirit of the church's consciousness of faith, that is, according to the norm of the *regula fidei,* and that all other exposition implies heretical departure from the church's consensus of faith, now, according to Gerhard Ebeling's formulation, the following principle applies:

> Holy Scripture is to be understood only through the Spirit through whom it was written and whom we encounter in no more contemporary, vital fashion than in the biblical text itself. The greater the danger of understanding the scripture according to

our own spirit, the more we must turn from all human writings to Holy Scripture alone. For there alone do we receive the Spirit who enables us to judge all scripture, pagan or Christian.[7]

If we go on to ask how this Spirit who carries scripture and enlightens us from it is to be defined, referring, for example, to Luther's explanation of the Third Article in the Small Catechism, we can only reply: The Spirit is the faith-initiating function of the gospel of justification, that gospel which is drawn from scripture and conferred in the oral proclamation. Faith is thus not a human performance but a human deed of hearing and obeying, initiated by God himself through the gospel, and only this faith shares salvation. Consequently, all Christian-churchly existence rests on the proclamation of Christ the sole Redeemer, a proclamation drawn from scripture alone and addressed to faith alone.

The Priority of Exegesis

Within the horizon of the so-called exclusive particles just introduced—*solus Christus, sola scriptura,* and *sola fide*—which belong together and cannot be separated, the task of scripture exposition in the Reformation can be unequivocally and clearly fixed: Exposition must be an exegesis applied to the scriptural texts which traces out the gospel and serves its preaching. Rather than relinquishing to the teaching office of the church the definition and summary of the many-layered witness of scripture to the one truth of faith, exegesis must now discover the gospel on its own. It can do so only when it dares to be an exegesis appropriate to its object, that is, an exposition which in converse with the biblical texts distinguishes gospel from law, the central proclamation of faith from what is peripheral and obscure. To the degree that the church's entire existence depends on the testimony and consolation of the gospel, a gospel to be drawn from scripture alone, exegesis of Holy Scripture appropriate to its object moves quite naturally from the rank of an adjunct discipline to the really dominant, chief theological task in the Reformation churches.

7. Gerhard Ebeling, " 'Sola scriptura' und das Problem der Tradition," *Das Neue Testament als Kanon,* ed. Ernst Käsemann (Göttingen: Vandenhoeck & Ruprecht, 1970), p. 315, in reference to D. Martin Luthers Werke. Kritische Gesamtausgabe (Weimar, 1883–   ), 7:97, 1–3, 11–13.

Exegetical Method

Understandably, this new, theologically central position given to scripture interpretation at once had consequences for method. It is not merely that Luther and Calvin—the one as pioneer, the other as theoretician and brilliant executor of Reformation exegesis—make Humanism's philological interest their own, and reach back of the Vulgate to the original biblical texts. Allegory is also evicted from its place as the dominant method. Now an exegetical method is needed which first of all facilitates return to and theological penetration of the original meaning of Holy Scripture.

In the wake of this need, Luther more and more abandoned allegory and established research into the literal meaning of scripture as the decisive exegetical task. At the same time, for Luther the old hermeneutical distinction between spirit and letter gives way to a new differentiation between law and gospel as the twofold function of the one word of God. Luther distinguishes a twofold clarity in scripture: the clarity and perspicuity of the outward, philologically analyzable meaning of the text, and the inner clarity at the gospel-heart of the scripture which cannot be reached without the aid of the Spirit. Outer and inner clarity are so united that the outwardly clear and plainly stated gospel of justification can only by the power of God's will subdue and free the sinner's conscience for faith. Conversely, they are so united that no proclamation of the gospel which sets out in faith from the heart of the scripture can neglect the biblical formulation. Rather, that proclamation has its decisive warranty in the philological clarity and perspicuity of the text.

Calvin then rejects allegory on principle and in his grand Bible commentaries devotes himself exclusively to clarifying the literal sense of the biblical books. With his doctrine of the *testimonium spiritus sancti internum,* that is, of the power of the biblical word which penetrates the heart solely by the divine working of the Spirit, he brings the Reformation doctrine of the Spirit into a simple, exegetically usable form: The exegetical and historical attempt to illumine the scripture's literal sense is subordinate to the working of the word as instrument of the Spirit. In other words, for Reformation exegesis, the task of the historical illumination of the text is to prepare for theological exegesis by way of clarification, and without being an end in itself.

If we see this, then we also understand—harking back to our initial reflections on Reformation interpretation—that the Reformers cannot expound the Holy Scripture simply by overleaping the tradition in favor of the original text and its time. Rather, they intend to interpret in a fashion conscious of the tradition. Proceeding from the original meaning of the texts, they aim at a reflective theological dialogue with the historical and dogmatic tradition of the church, a tradition in part instructive and in part also full of error and miscalculation. The goal of the entire hermeneutical enterprise is to lift out the original gospel of Christ within and for the church so as to making a binding proclamation of this gospel a possibility for the present.

The Exegetical Goal

In the place of ancient church and medieval allegory with its ascent of knowledge, the Reformation brings a theological exposition of scripture, which is discriminating in respect of its content, rooted in history, and emphatically concerned for the original meaning of scripture. The goal of the exegetical procedure is to facilitate the preaching of the gospel. The exegete no longer ascends from the word of the scripture to eternal rest in God, but traces the incarnate mission of Jesus Christ in human history and comes to a kerygmatic encounter and confrontation of gospel, church, and world. Reformation exegesis makes totally its own the traditional hermeneutical experience of the spiritual understanding of scripture. But instead of congealing scripture, church, and a common perception of truth with the aid of allegory, an interpretation of scripture now emerges which directs its chief attention to the biblical witness to history and leads to encounter with the biblical gospel.

If in this sense all of Christian existence is wagered on the theological process of scripture interpretation, from now on the existence of the Reformation churches must depend on the degree of their success with such historical and theological exegesis. The Reformation churches were not spared stagnation, oversimplification, and aberration, though in and despite all their new model of exposition was theologically and historically far more productive than allegory, which was no longer suited to the rapidly and totally changing historical consciousness.

EXEGESIS FOLLOWING THE REFORMATION

Keeping chiefly to the development of the hermeneutical problem in Protestantism, great changes occur from the end of the sixteenth century onward, and against the background of profound cultural, political, and social upheavals in all of Europe. We will trace only a few of the critical stages.

Protestant Orthodoxy

First of all, under the weight of controversy with Catholicism the pioneering exegesis of the Reformation is again completely absorbed by dogmatics, especially in Protestant Orthodoxy. For Orthodoxy biblical exegesis is in essence only an auxiliary discipline which prepares "proof texts" from the biblical canon for the dogmatic system. Of special consequence was the orthodox refinement of the doctrine of inspiration to the point where Holy Scripture is inspired both as to inner content and external wording, and thus implies and facilitates a closed system of Christian doctrine. This drafting of the doctrine of dictation (*Theopneustia*) had signal results because it no longer allowed a free and critical scrutiny of the original biblical text, to say nothing of an encounter of the historical utterances of scripture with the dogmatic system. In other words, armed with this concept of the doctrine of inspiration Orthodoxy was obliged to shield itself from a free historical investigation and evaluation of the biblical texts and writings. It had to protect itself against a Reformation return to the original meaning of the scripture to the degree such return implied a principle criticism of the urgency and rigor of its own confessional system.

The Emergence of Historical-Critical Research

The historical results of this narrowing were not long in coming. Due to the obduracy of Orthodoxy as sketched above,

Pietism and Christian Free Thought together emerged to assert the possibility of a free new encounter and occupation with the Bible. In making common cause against Orthodoxy, the fixing of goals—vastly different in the two camps—was for a time postponed and the way paved for what we today call the historical-critical research of the Bible.

A glance at Philip Jacob Spener's (1635–1705) famed *Pia Desideria* best illustrates what was cardinal in Pietism. In conscious dependence on Luther, Pietism's intention was to encounter the scriptural word anew, in order from that point to refine and deepen Christian faith and life within the circle of the brotherhood. The orthodox doctrine, honed to a fine point in theological debate and rationally articulated in the grand manner, did not achieve this refinement. Pietism's bold, critical research into the original biblical text; the revival of knowledge of the biblical languages, Hebrew and Greek; and the equally daring move toward scientific discussion of the original meaning of the Old and New Testament writings served—as the examples of August Hermann Francke and Johann Albrecht Bengel indicate—this encounter with scripture in its pure originality, an encounter which revived the insight and missionary courage of faith. Though the historical-critical enterprise served faith in this manner and thus for Pietism was from the outset a means to an end in the true sense of the word, Francke and Bengel had to suffer harshest criticism from the church for their procedure.[8]

THE ENLIGHTENMENT

The bitterness of the debates in that period is indicated by the fact that in 1730, Johann Jakob Wettstein—at first a theological representative of moderate Orthodoxy—was actually relieved of his pulpit at Basel due to his text-critical studies on the New Testament, specifically for his alleged opposition to the church's confession.

This event also explains why in the period following historical-critical research was chiefly and almost on principle carried on in

---

8. See Martin Brecht, "Johann Albrecht Bengels Theologie der Schrift," *ZThK* 64 (1967): 106.

opposition to all dogmatic tradition and supervision in the church. In Protestantism, Johann Salomo Semler (1725–91) paved the way for this type of historical criticism which set itself the goal of investigating the biblical canon and its writings, free of all clerical censure and independent of the claims and inherited stating of issues in church tradition. Such criticism could in a measure be construed as an act of the Protestant spirit and at the same time as a service to Christian faith, since it was assumed almost without question that the spirit of the rational, enlightened, and morally engaged religion of the time was also the Spirit of the New Testament, and of Jesus above all. Thus the experiences of virtually the entire ancient, Reformation, and Orthodox teaching on the Spirit were set aside in favor of an hermeneutical identification of the individual's own religious and enlightened pre-understanding with New Testament ideas of the Spirit.

As is well known, this synthesis was broken only at the end of the last century, in Hermann Gunkel's famous essay on "Die Wirkungen des heiligen Geistes nach der populären Anschauung der apostolischen Zeit und nach der Lehre des Apostels Paulus," and with the arrival of the so-called history of religions school. Under the aegis of this synthesis—which appears untenable to us today—began a historical research of the Bible which incredibly deepened and enriched our knowledge of the origin, varied content, and history of the biblical books. No contemporary theologian can forego the results and experience-data of this methodological biblical criticism, in use since the eighteenth century.

The Problem of the Canon

Still, the new emergent also had its problems, whose consequences we trace and must bear even today. They are manifest first of all in the treatment of the biblical canon itself. In the name of rational Christianity, Old and New Testaments were now pitted against each other in a manner unlike that experienced in the church since Marcion. Enlightened religiosity defended itself against the spirit of the Old Testament and began to classify the Old Testament literature as evidence of a pre-Christian, Jewish religion, and thus to disparage its content.

Semler writes that he is not morally improved by the twenty-

four books of the Old Testament canon, and believes the Old
Testament consists "of a collection of crude Jewish prejudices
diametrically opposed to Christianity." He concludes that "a
wholesome extract from the books of the Old Testament would
more easily and convincingly commend the Christian teaching
and religion to experience than the cold repetitions of facts, which
to us and our taste in science and morals are and remain thoroughly outlandish, totally alien, and obscure."[9] Semler's appraisal
is not unique. Schleiermacher's conviction that "in its progress,
vital Christianity needs no support whatever from Judaism," was
as old as his religious consciousness itself.[10] Schleiermacher
found that the Old Testament fostered among Christians a "legal-
istic type thought" or "servitude to the letter," and preferred to
see it ranked as a mere appendage to the New Testament so as
to meet the requirement "that the whole Old Testament first be
worked through in order properly to arrive at the New."[11] And
Adolf von Harnack's famous verdict read:

> Rejection of the Old Testament in the second century was an
> error the Great Church rightly refused; to retain it in the six-
> teenth century was a fate the Reformation was not yet able to
> avert; but to preserve it as canonical record in Protestantism since
> the nineteenth century is the result of a religious and ecclesiasti-
> cal paralysis. . . . The great feat required of Protestantism today
> —almost too late—is to make a clean sweep here and in confession
> and instruction to honor truth.[12]

These statements are all typical of an evaluation of the Old
Testament in the wake of historical criticism which Old Testament study to this moment must struggle to overcome.

The Autonomy of Biblical Criticism

These examples make clear that a historical criticism of the
biblical literature which is unchecked and abandons all experience of tradition and dogmatics in the church can develop an
autonomy which allows irreconcilable fronts to emerge between

9. Quoted from Hans-Joachim Kraus, *Geschichte der historisch-kritischen
Erforschung des Alten Testaments*, 2te Auflage (Neukirchen-Vluyn: Neukirchener Verlag, 1969), p. 109–10.
10. See ibid., p. 171.
11. Ibid., pp. 172–73.
12. Ibid., p. 386.

scientific insight on the one hand and vital Christian faith on the other. What is the cause?

The attack on Christianity by Hermann Samuel Reimarus (1694–1768), the "Anonymous Wolfenbütteler" championed by Lessing, an attack spun in a critical, rationalistic temper from out of a fanciful analysis of the synoptic Gospels, was not entirely unforeseen in the age of deism and the Enlightenment. But it signalized most clearly how little the system of historical criticism invokes a specifically Christian method, or even a method tailored to the needs of Christian theology. It rather entails a method which European historiography, flourishing since the seventeenth century, created by fits and starts in order to expose all historical tradition to the gaze and access of critical reason, a method subject only to the criteria of reason. Fastening upon texts of the past in uninhibited, rational fashion thus serves the dual purpose of setting free and initiating a new communication with the truth. It sets free from the pressure and compulsion of a clerical tradition, still undisputed in value but now felt to inhibit freedom, and initiates a genuine communication with the truth, since according to the Enlightenment view, reason is manifest in the thought of single historical individuals and in the forward progress of history as a whole.

In the eighteenth and nineteenth centuries German Protestantism resolved to appropriate this critical system of knowledge, which for the history of science yielded an interesting constellation of parallels to the second and third centuries. Then, the ancient church had decided to adapt for Christian use the allegorical method originally shaped by the Stoa, an adaptation made feasible by the then prevailing identification of the Stoic-Platonic world-reason with Christ in the Logos-idea. Now, historical criticism was adopted under the aegis of a synthesis of revelation and reason in the notion of a rational religion and in a view of history as the upward moral development of mankind. The gain in knowledge was no greater than the price to be paid for that novel synthesis.

We have just spoken of the increment in knowledge which to this day cannot be ignored. But the price consists not only in a critical dissection of the biblical canon, but above all in the fact that for a very long time contact between the church's dogmatic tradition and scientific-critical theology was broken off. Communication between scientific theology and the church of believers was interrupted and Protestantism was faced with the question as to how far it could participate in current developments and reject inherited elements of the tradition without losing its Christian identity. A historical alternative to the course of Protestant theology was not then and is not now in sight. The fact that Catholicism today has upheld the Protestant verdict in favor of historical criticism, a criticism it once supposed it should and could reject, actually best vindicates the Protestant course of action. But in my opinion there is no reason to overestimate this course, because that bold resolve on behalf of historical criticism has most heavily burdened and still oppresses the church of the Reformation, dependent as no other on the capability and effectiveness of its theological interpretation of scripture.

THE NINETEENTH CENTURY

Naturally, Protestant theology did not go this way blindly. Throughout the entire nineteenth century it intensively probed the historical and hermeneutical problematic which faced it, and did not avoid the risk of painful aberrations.

Strauss

As to aberrations, I simply call to mind the fate of the Tübingen tutor, David Friedrich Strauss (1808–74). He intended to do justice both to radical historical criticism and to the claim of the Christian faith, first by subjecting the Gospel record of Jesus' career and fate to a historical criticism which his time regarded as unsparing, then by classifying the peculiarly Christian data of faith such as the Incarnation, resurrection, and ascension of Jesus as pregnant mythical ideas whose historical orgin can be traced and thus in good conscience appropriated as concepts born of faith. The church of his day regarded this solution as so untenable that it removed Strauss from his tutorship and later at Zurich did not allow him to take up the professorship which had been tendered him. The further course of Strauss' thought, critical of the church and naturally not uninfluenced by these events, indicates that his attempt still did not create any generally viable connection between faith and biblical criticism, but rather marked a setting of the hermeneutical task to which each succeeding theological generation must address itself.

Baur

With respect to the historical effectiveness of critical and theological exposition, no Protestant can ignore the pioneering work of Ferdinand Christian Baur (1792–1860). His work is characterized first of all by the fact that, unlike his pupil David Friedrich Strauss, Baur was not obliged to force apart the historical and theological concerns of exegesis, but could connect them on the basis of his idea of history. According to Baur, the exegete, in the very performance of his historical-critical study, catches sight of the essentially theological content of his text, since history is the movement of the divine Spirit itself. For this reason, in exacting work with the historical witness of the scripture the interpreter can note and retrace the self-witness of the divine Spirit.

Even today we can see from Baur's work to what extent the productivity of historical criticism is dependent on the view of history assumed at any given time. This is especially true of historical criticism in the area of theology. If the concept of history here is too narrow to allow a disclosure by way of revelation (of whatever kind) historical-critical results must of necessity oppose the gospel's revelatory claim. Conversely, if historical criticism operates with a view of history and reality which is open to transcendence, it can glean essential data for the orientation of church and preaching.

Awareness of this functionalism in method should not lead us to forget that an interpreter cannot choose his view of history and reality simply of his own accord. He must always take it over from his time in order, as far as possible, to identify with it or oppose it. In other words, no historical-critical interpretation can avoid being embedded in its time. Precisely because it must always assume a certain notion of reality for its interpretation, it is itself always an historical phenomenon.

The Hermeneutical Dilemma

We are thus confronted with the hermeneutical dilemma of historical criticism—originally setting out under the twofold premise that history, as other world phenomena, is objectifiable to a study which is thoroughgoing as to method, and that it is precisely historical method which can guarantee such an objective study of history, free of judgment and prejudice. In nineteenth century occupation with hermeneutics the ideal of historical method's freedom from judgment or bias and the notion of an objective, naturalistic study of history proved to be simplifications.

Since history together with its records is a specifically human life-expression, it can only be understood and interpreted when viewed as a complex life-expression. But such a view assumes the interpreter is capable of sharing the life and feeling of his given historical counterpart. Thus, beyond describing and illumining facts and texts, a truly penetrating study of history implies a psychological and even divinatory aspect.

These insights, which we owe first of all to Schleiermacher and Wilhelm Dilthey, lead, in conjunction with the idealistic study of history known to us from Baur, to an evaluation of the preeminence of religious personality in history. In its religious intuition the personality is the historical medium of transcendence. Together with its decisions, it also determines the course of history. In this dual role personality is a hermeneutically indispensable key, and precisely for a theological study of history. Because the divine Spirit and historically illuminable reality coincide in the self-consciousness of the religious individual, the scientific and theological concerns can be joined and reconciled in the evaluation and description of religious personality, its intention, and fate.

Since this was so, the nineteenth century, taken as a whole, could successfully reject all attempts to develop a special theological hermeneutic for the interpretation of the biblical writings —which of course removes theology from the claim of universal scientific accountability, but at the same time amounts to a rupture of rational communication between the church's proclamation and the perception of historical reality.

We must respect and welcome this development with its insights, though we know today that the idealistic view of history, the concept of religious personality, and the synthesis of spirit and reality which each assumed have lost their integrating power with the passage of time.

THE TURN OF THE CENTURY

We immediately note this loss of power when we try to sketch the impasse to which critical Protestant theology came at the beginning of our century. Reduced to a simple scheme, the situation can be characterized by three men—Franz Overbeck, Ernst Troeltsch, and Adolf Schlatter. All three represent a distinct view of the rigor and necessity of historical criticism in theology.

Overbeck

Franz Overbeck, from 1870 Professor of New Testament and Ancient Church History at Basel, represents a type of radical historical critic whose analysis of New Testament texts and events breaks the connection between scripture and church. Indeed, Overbeck breaks that connection to such degree that he accuses all theological exegesis seeking to fix lines of communication between scripture and church of a timid or brazen allegorizing which illicitly minimizes the aggravating fact of the collapse of the imminent expectation in primitive Christianity. Faced with these alternatives, Overbeck chooses the path of criticism or, as he himself says, of unbelief, surrenders his chair in 1897, and publicly champions theses he had withheld from his students while a theological teacher. Thus for Overbeck, radical historical criticism bars access to the tradition of the church and to a contemporary faith lived from out of scripture.

Troeltsch

The argument of Ernst Troeltsch, the great systematician of theological liberalism and historicism, is an entirely different matter. In his essay, "Über historische und dogmatische Methode in der Theologie," first appearing in 1898,[13] he offers a thus

13. Cf. Ernst Troeltsch, *Theologie als Wissenschaft*, ed. Gerhard Sauter, *ThB* 43 (1971): 105–27.

far unexcelled explanation of the structure of historical criticism. At the same time, as in all of his work, he urges that in awareness of its historical situation theology must strike its tent once more, overcome its dogmatic-supernaturalistic tradition, and cooperate in a comprehensive historical-cultural synthesis of religion, morality, reason, and humanity. If we keep more clearly in mind Troeltsch's methodological analysis of historical criticism, we can properly understand his argument.

According to Troeltsch, historical criticism operates with three indissolubly connected principles. He calls them criticism, analogy, and correlation. Criticism denotes a systematic skepticism which the historian applies without partiality to all historical tradition. This criticism is made possible by analogy, that is, the assumption of an intrinsic similarity in all historical occurrence. Troeltsch speaks emphatically of the "omnipotence" and "all-leveling purport" of analogy,[14] because it embraces all present and past historical occurrence in a single context of events, allows no arbitrary establishment of occurrences or revelatory texts without analogy, and enables the interpreter to make contemporary historical phenomena which are directly known and familiar to him the interpretative framework and criterion for comparable events in the past. The third principle, of correlation, that is, of the coherence and reciprocal action of historical events, is indeed already given with the concept of analogy, but now where expressly named, it prevents arbitrary criticism or use of the scheme of analogy. It compels the historian to range his individual findings within the entire structure of historical events and thus scientifically to examine them. Troeltsch thus totally disallows isolated, untested critical hypotheses.

When by means of an historical criticism working with these three principles the theological tradition is set once for all within the entire course of historical occurrence, much, indeed everything, depends on how this coherence of events is ontologically conceived. With the needed clarity, Troeltsch responds that he can urge us to put historical-critical study into practice in theology (and for him that means embracing the idea of a universal theology in the history of religion) only because he does not

14. Ibid., p. 108.

regard history as sheer chaos. On the contrary, "faith in a reason which prevails and progressively reveals itself in history" is an "indispensable presupposition" for his train of thought.[15] Thus for Troeltsch, the framework for historical criticism is a concept of universal history stamped by German idealism and culture-optimism. This view then enables him to speak of new and pioneering events within the course of history, that is, when the bearer and initiator of such novelties is the individual open to transcendence—that "religious personality"[16] which we met earlier. In contrast to Overbeck, Troeltsch regards historical criticism as that method above all which points theology the way to the future because it enables theology with its treasure of religious experience to share in a universal historical progress and in its own way even to help give it shape.

Schlatter

As fascinating and, to a degree, even attractive as this notion is, Adolf Schlatter did not allow this liberal program to blind him to the fact that the historical-critical method involves a procedure the implications of which are theologically of great import and highly problematic. Rather, he passionately resisted measuring the scientific character of theology simply by whether and to what degree it appropriates this prefabricated historical-critical type procedure. At the same time, he most urgently pleaded that the exegete not merely allow his method of handling the biblical tradition to be given him ready-made, but let it take shape only through honest study of his objects and texts. To the extent he does this, according to Schlatter, he is a scientist.

> The duty absolutely binding on us as members of the community of learning is that in the area of study allotted us we come to a seeing, to a chaste and pure observation, to a grasping of the actual event, whether happened or happening. This is the obligation of all university study. Science is first, second, third, and

15. Ibid., p. 121.
16. On the significance of the religious individual in Troeltsch, see Eckard Lessing, *Die Geschichtsphilosophie Ernst Troeltschs* (Hamburg-Bergstedt: Reich Verlag, 1965), pp. 82–89, 94–99; and Ernst Wilhelm Kohls, "Das Bild der Reformation bei Wilhelm Dilthey, Adolf von Harnack und Ernst Troeltsch," *ZSTh* 11 (1969): 286–87.

always a seeing. Nothing exempts us from this calling, whatever
takes place in other areas of scientific work. . . . The results of
our colleagues' study may have the greatest significance for us;
they may create problems fraught with deepest, even impenetrable obscurity: the theologian is obliged to grasp the area of
occurrence entrusted to him with a resolute devotion to his own
object.[17]

Or, more critically put and with a view to his own New Testament discipline and guild:

At present, historical literature on the New Testament is over-
loaded with conjectures offered to us as history. The cause of this
state of affairs is not merely that we fail to see, and engage in
fantasy instead of seeing, but also that the historian gives no
account of the motives which impel him, and takes the absence of
historical presuppositions in his field as license indiscriminately
to overlook the presuppositions which govern him personally. We
are freed from our presuppositions and lifted above them only
when we are keenly conscious of them.[18]

In other words, Schlatter argues for a critical exchange of
theological history with historical method as such, and with this
requirement recovers on a scientific level the old interest of
Pietism in a merely instrumental use of historical criticism. If,
after noting this, we mistakenly assume that Schlatter was concerned with an uncritical exegesis, we must immediately add that
on the contrary, he urges a theological exegesis after the Reformation pattern. He even expressly refers to the exegete's right
and duty to form his own considered judgment on what he has
observed. Since Schlatter's position and his criticism of liberalism is too little known, though it anticipates essential elements
of the protest of dialectical theology against liberal theology, we
quote once more word for word:

We can never give past occurrence absolute power to shape us, so
that the telling of what was could render our judgment super-
fluous, or tradition replace our own reflection, or norms moving
our wills from without replace our own volition. We are always
called to an act of reflection, in which our own personality forms

17. Adolf Schlatter, "Atheistische Methoden in der Theologie," in *Zur
Theologie des Neuen Testaments und zur Dogmatik, Kleine Schriften,* ed.
Ulrich Luck, *ThB* 41 (1969): 142.
18. Schlatter, "Die Theologie des Neuen Testaments und die Dogmatik," in
ibid., p. 213.

its judgment. That is an axiom of biblical, or . . . in any event, of evangelical piety.[19]

Schlatter is thus concerned for a critical theology with a biblical basis. He sets historical criticism in the service of this theological concern and requires of the theologian a capacity for dealing critically with his own method. But Schlatter does not require a special, spiritual hermeneutic. On his view biblical exegesis must rather remain an historical science, even when its object yields special hermeneutical problems which it must resolve by itself.

Liberalism and the History-of-Religions School

When we look backward an interesting panorama emerges. Three ways of initiating historical criticism dominate: the radical criticism of Overbeck, which breaks with theology; Troeltsch's program of a history-of-religions theology rooted in a thoroughgoing historical criticism; and finally the theological criticism of historical method already present in Schlatter.

It is clear from the beginning that a choice favorable to theology could only be made between the positions represented by Troeltsch and Schlatter. Since Schlatter defended his theses in a manner not easily accessible from the viewpoint of language and content, since he was known to be a partisan of conservative circles in the church, and since he was not prepared fully to test the possibilities of free historical reflection within the framework of his theological system, Troeltsch and liberalism gained wide theological interest up to the moment the two critical supports in its program gave way: first, the synthesis of the biblical idea of Spirit and religious-anthropological self-consciousness, and second, the culture-optimistic idea of history. The first shattered when history-of-religions research into Old and New Testaments demonstrated the disparity between the Bible's dynamic concept of Spirit and modern anthropological self-consciousness, and when hope in a cultural evolution in and through history was dashed for a long time to come by the experiences of the First World War. The way was thus open for dialectical theology's attempt at reform.

19. Schlatter, "Atheistische Methoden in der Theologie," pp. 138–39.

DIALECTICAL THEOLOGY

When in the course of our reflections on historical-critical exposition we wish to describe the decisive hermeneutical impulse of dialectical theology, we must emphasize that Karl Barth and Rudolf Bultmann—in our context the two key figures among the dialecticians—were both intent on giving new value to the Reformers' hermeneutical impulse. They did so in a situation in which the christological and kerygmatic identity of church and theology was in danger of being completely lost in a culture-synthesis, the force of which was already spent. But Barth and Bultmann attached themselves to the Reformation and its understanding of the gospel in a situation which is new in the history of theology. They do not aim simply at repristinating the old, but at giving a new and critical account of Reformation tradition in the present. This means that both had especially to come to terms with the phenomenon and effectiveness of historical criticism.

It is highly interesting to note the course of this debate, since Barth in so many words refers to Calvin's view of scripture together with his doctrine of the *testimonium spiritus sancti internum,* intending to give new value to this doctrine. Bultmann, on the other hand, comes from the Lutheran tradition for which the word of God in the true sense is only the oral, preached gospel, and for which the true working of the Spirit must be assigned and granted only to this orally proclaimed kerygma.

Barth

Barth, an exegete only in the systematic sense and above all a Reformed dogmatician, opens the debate in the prefaces to the first three editions of his Romans commentary and in his famous open correspondence with Adolf von Harnack.[20] With the programmatic warning, "the critical historians need to be more critical!"[21] Barth calls for a reasoned out, instrumental use of

20. All these publications are included in the second, enlarged edition of the volume *Anfänge der dialektischen Theologie* 1, ed. Jürgen Moltmann, *ThB* 17 (1966).
21. The preface to the second edition of Karl Barth, *The Epistle to the Romans,* trans. Edwyn C. Hoskyns (London: Oxford University Press, 1950), p. 8.

historical criticism in the service and interest of a theological interpretation which penetrates beyond historical analyses. Though to this day exegetes and historians regard Barth as an enemy of historical criticism, he himself did not intend to be such. He rather demanded and practised what Rudolf Smend has suggestively and happily termed a "post-critical exposition of scripture,"[22] that is, a Bible interpretation which does not stay with or mire down in historical-critical problems, but penetrates through them to the revelatory witness which shines from scripture.

We can get an exact picture of Barth's hermeneutical concern from two of his later utterances on our theme. In 1968, in the postscript to his Schleiermacher anthology, Barth records his own experiences with historical criticism. He writes in frank fashion: "At that time I unlearned what makes the flesh crawl. I so thoroughly went through the historical-critical school of the older sort that the remarks of its later and current disciples could no longer get under my skin or even at my heart, but, as is too well known, only on my nerves."[23] In his farewell lecture at Basel in the winter semester of 1961–62, published under the title *Evangelical Theology: An Introduction,* and one of the most beautiful books Barth ever wrote, he gives extensive information concerning his view of post-critical exegesis. There he states:

> The science of biblical theology does not work in empty space but in the service of the community of Jesus Christ, which is founded by prophetic and apostolic testimony. It is precisely for this reason that it approaches these texts with a specific *expectation.* (Nothing more than this should be said, but also nothing less!). Biblical theology expects that testimony to the God who calls for faith will confront it in these texts. Nevertheless, it remains unreservedly open to such questions as: Will this expectation be fulfilled? (This is precisely what is involved in the so-called "hermeneutical circle.") To what extent, in what form, and through what concrete expressions will the uniqueness which these texts possess for the community confirm itself? Is such exegesis "dogmatic" exegesis? An affirmative answer has to be given only to the extent that the science of theological exegesis rejects, at the outset, every dogma which might forbid it the

22. Rudolf Smend, "Nachkritische Schriftauslegung," *Parrēsia.* Festschrift für Karl Barth zum 80. Geburtstag (Zollikon-Zürich: Evangelischer Verlag A.G., 1966), pp. 215–37.
23. *Schleiermacher Auswahl.* Mit einem Nachwort von Karl Barth (Munich: Siebenstern-Taschenbuch-Verlag, 1968), p. 291.

expectation just mentioned and might declare, from the very beginning, its vindication to be impossible. Again, is this "pneumatic" exegesis? Certainly not, in so far as such exegesis might
suppose it was able to dispose over the Scriptures on the basis of
some imagined spiritual power that it possesses. But it may be
called "pneumatic" to the extent that it uses the freedom, founded
upon the Scriptures themselves, to address to them seriously,
ultimately, and definitively a strict question about the Spirit's own
testimony heard in them.[24]

With Calvin's view of scripture in mind, we cannot construe
Barth's use of the slogan "pneumatic exegesis" in terms of an
arbitrary and unsystematic application of scripture, but must speak
of a reattachment to critical dimensions of exegesis in the ancient
church and the Reformation.

Still, its secure position in the history of theology cannot pre-
vent our referring to the problem in Barth's hermeneutic, particularly—as stressed at the outset—from the viewpoint of the
exegete. Barth's conception of the principle of revelation, and
his opposition to an exclusively historical-critical analysis of the
text hindered him from seeing the hermeneutical problem in its
full breadth. They prevented him from outlining a method which
would have been useful also to the professional exegete, enabling
the exegete actually to reach the theological dimension of interpretation which Barth demanded, while threading his way
through the historical task of text analysis. When it is said that
Barth's purpose was not to elaborate such an outline we must
respect the fact that at that time exegesis, bound to its scientific-
historical setting of the task as well as to the theological task of
interpretation, could not directly follow Barth's stimulus, but
sought to make its own hermeneutical way between historicism
and the new dialectical beginning. And with that we have arrived at Rudolf Bultmann.

Bultmann

Bultmann's exegetical, hermeneutical, and theological work
was so decisive for Protestant theology in the twentieth century
because he was able to achieve and openly demonstrate what
Barth appeared only to postulate: an integration of thorough-

24. Karl Barth, *Evangelical Theology: An Introduction*, trans. Grover Foley
(New York: Rinehart and Winston, 1963), pp. 177–78.

going historical criticism and kerygmatic theology in the service of the church. Add to this the pregnancy and clarity of Bultmann's train of thought, the powerful academic effect of which the Tübingen faculty called to public attention in its opinion on Bultmann's theology in March of 1952,[25] and which Eberhard Jüngel has only recently reemphasized.[26]

Bultmann aimed at this hermeneutical integration by conceding to radical historical criticism and the preached kerygma their full right. In his outline for an existential interpretation he combined the historical and kerygmatic concerns for scripture in a methodologically useful way. This interpretative combination, reminiscent of the attempt of David Friedrich Strauss, was facilitated by a view of history which dismissed the puzzling question as to the meaning and teleology of all history, a question which liberalism clearly could not solve, and in its place inquired into the individual's encounter with historical events, and sought to illumine the significance and the structure of this encounter. This type of historical study, which Bultmann by no means one-sidedly borrowed from Heidegger, but developed independently in dialogue with him, is linked to the earlier idealistic and historical view of history. In both, the individual, open to transcendence and functioning, so to speak, as its historical agent, represents the key figure in which historically demonstrable reality and reality which can only be religiously experienced encounter each other. That Bultmann, just as idealism, always defines the individual—in preference to all other definitions of existence—as a being with a conscious relation to itself,[27] supports our linking the ideal type of religious personality in idealism or historicism with the existence of the individual in this new existential view of history.

25. "Für und wider die Theologie Bultmanns," SGV 198/199 (1952): 38. The discussion is in essence the work of Hanns Rückert, and is now easily available in his Vorträge und Aufsätze zur historischen Theologie (Tübingen: J. C. B. Mohr, 1972), pp. 404–33, especially p. 428.
26. Eberhard Jüngel, "Redlich von Gott reden: Bemerkungen zur Klarheit der Theologie Rudolf Bultmanns," Ev Komm 7 (1974): 475–77.
27. This can be most clearly seen in Bultmann's structural analysis of the Pauline concept of the body, Theology of the New Testament, trans. Kendrick Grobel (London: SCM Press, 1952), 1: 195–96. According to Bultmann, "man is called soma in respect to his being able to make himself the object of his own action or to experience himself as the subject to whom something happens. He can be called soma, that is, as having a relationship to himself." (The entire passage is italicized.)

In practice, the study of history and the New Testament under existential presuppositions means critically to view and test what events and transmissions of the historical tradition affect the individual's existence here and now, calling him into question or to new dimensions of life. But since from the time of the Reformation the essential theological question is, What does the gospel say, how does it as preached word affect the individual, and how does it call him into question or to new dimensions of life? the existential, critical analysis of the text and Reformation-theological concern for scripture cannot only be combined, but in essence actually coincide, provided we agree with Bultmann's third assumption. This assumption is the truly dialectical element in Bultmann's theology, and in turn touches some essential features in Luther's theology: Man must submit to the injunction against desiring to make God, his work, and his word directly an item of objectifying research. Rather, man preserves God's honor and his freedom of action when he seeks to grasp the divine activity only in its historical results, above all, in the mirror of believing existence seized by the word and will of God.

If we make this third assumption and allow it as a theologically legitimate position, then in the existential analysis of the New Testament—and we might add of the Old Testament and church tradition as a whole—the historical-critical concern, focused on existence, and the Reformation theological interest in the biblical word come together in almost ideal fashion. Historical criticism is actually at one with theological criticism insofar as historical criticism prevents faith from binding itself to objects other than God's present activity in the word alone, whether those objects be in the form of ambiguous historical saving facts or earlier mythological interpretations of the gospel. Thus also for Bultmann, historical criticism is not simply a liberating end in itself, but a tool of theological reflection, since in its formulation of the question which tests, explains, and renders everything doubtful, it leaves faith ultimately to itself, that is, solely dependent on God's word. Only when we see how Bultmann intends to bring faith to consciousness by his critical, existential interpretation of the biblical texts, can we understand his bold statement that his program of existential interpretation, that is, of demythologizing the New

Testament, is "the radical application of the doctrine of justification by faith to the sphere of knowledge and thought."[28] In Bultmann's hermeneutical method the concerns of the exegete and the Lutheran theologian have struck an ideal unity—to be sure, under the conditions of the modern, or more precisely, existential analysis of human existence (*Dasein*).

We can even go a step further. Within the framework of Luther's and of Paul's theology, the individual is a decisive category, since it is the individual who stands alone before his God and is accepted and freed by him in justification. In Paul and in Luther the individual is thus an eschatological category given with the gospel of justification. Once we note this we can even attempt to relax Bultmann's alliance with and affinity for existential philosophy and say that a theological study of history as such must pay special heed to the existence of the individual, and that accordingly Bultmann's combination of hermeneutical methods is, in itself, theologically correct. We can also say that to upset that combination would be to attack the Reformation view of faith, the gospel, and the individual singled out by the gospel. Walter Schmithals and Günter Klein are presently moving toward such an assessment of Bultmann's hermeneutics.[29] But in my opinion, they are in danger of making an historical system of knowledge, limited in its productivity, into a theory of theological interpretation valid for its own sake.

With this sketch we have already arrived at the present day, but before we proceed directly to its problematic we must still consider the high cost of Bultmann's elegant system. In terms of history and hermeneutics, it consists in the fact that all New Testament traditions and utterances which do not automatically fit Bultmann's interpretative requirements are subject to historical as well as theological criticism. But these traditions and utterances—alongside the preaching of Jesus which Bultmann classifies as a mere presupposition for New Testament Christology—are

28. Rudolf Bultmann, *Jesus Christ And Mythology* (New York: Charles Scribner's Sons, 1958), p. 84. On this thesis of Bultmann, see also pp. 63–64 below.
29. See Walther Schmithals, "Barth, Bultmann und wir," *Ev Komm* 2 (1969): 447–452; and Günter Klein, "Rudolf Bultmann—ein Lehrer der Kirche," *DtPfBl* (1974, Heft 9): 1–4, with implicit and explicit criticism of my hermeneutical attempt in *ZThK* (1971).

quite essential portions of the christological kerygma and of the Christology detailed in the New Testament. They include, for example, statements regarding Jesus' atoning death, his being raised, his activity as risen Reconciler, and his Parousia. They also embrace the chief New Testament texts concerning cosmology and eschatology, and further, the New Testament view of a salvation-historical connection between Israel and the Christian community, or even the New Testament theology of creation. Note that Bultmann eliminates none of these texts and traditions from the Bible as from the outset irrelevant, but he is resolved, and forced, critically to inquire behind them all for their existential content and to measure them theologically by his conception of pure faith under the word. It is this position which automatically hinders Bultmann from a truly thorough evaluation of the Old Testament. It forces him to disparage all dogmatic reflection and formulation in the church which is more than an analysis of the Christian consciousness of faith, and to such extent that it can scarcely give the church—always highly prized by Bultmann—the needed assistance in thought and formulation for its faith and confession.

Taking all this into account, the theological and exegetical problematic in Bultmann's outline becomes clear, and it is conceivable why it is so difficult, even impossible for some to remain with Bultmann's system, while those who defend it must in future assume the heavy theological mortgage with which this hermeneutic is encumbered.

CATHOLIC HERMENEUTICS

Evaluation of the contemporary situation, however, includes familiarity not merely with the evolution of Protestant exegesis, but with Catholic hermeneutic as well. We conclude our historical survey with a quite terse sketch of its route from the Reformation to the present day.

First of all, in the sixteenth century Catholicism opposed the project for reform in Reformation exposition by elevating the inherited ecclesiastical system of interpretation to a dogmatic norm at the Council of Trent, and by tying itself to the canon of the Vulgate as the text binding judicially and in matters of morals. In 1546, the Council of Trent decreed:

> No one relying on his own judgment shall, in matters of faith and morals pertaining to the edification of Christian doctrine, distorting the Holy Scriptures in accordance with his own conceptions, presume to interpret them contrary to the sense which holy mother Church, to whom it belongs to judge of their true sense and interpretation, has held and holds, or even contrary to the unanimous teaching of the Fathers, even though such interpretations should never at any time be published.[30]

The result of this decree was that the beginnings of historical-critical research on the text and tradition of scripture were suppressed for a long time to come. Even Richard Simon of the French oratory (1638–1712), who with his historical-critical writings on the Old Testament and on the text and early exposition of the New Testament aimed to attack and document the indefensibility of the orthodox Protestant doctrine of inspiration, and prove that in view of the history of the Bible's text and interpretation the truth of religion is guaranteed only by the teaching church, was thrust out of his order and the reading of his writings proscribed. Only now does the Catholic church remember him as a pioneer of critical historical work from its own ranks and in the seventeenth century as a whole.

The fundamental hermeneutical decision made at Trent was underscored at the First Vatican Council in 1870 and given the finishing touch by the proclamation of papal infallibility in doctrinal decisions. Up to this time and for a generation to come the venture in hermeneutics and the leadership in the area of critical exegesis lay clearly with the Protestants, until after long and painful struggle the Catholic church decided to recognize the necessity of the historical-critical investigation of scripture in the service of faith and the church. The three major documents in this connection are the papal encyclical *Divino afflante Spiritu* of September 30, 1943; the papal biblical commission's *Instructio de historica Evangeliorum veritate* of April 21, 1964; and finally the Second Vatican Council's Constitution on the Word of God,

30. *Canons And Decrees Of The Council Of Trent*, original text with English translation, Henry Joseph Schroeder, O.P. (London: B. Herder Book Co., 1955), pp. 18–19.

Dei Verbum, of November 18, 1965. These documents continue
to maintain that the Catholic church is founded upon scripture
and tradition; that scripture, tradition, and church are united in
the doctrine of inspiration, and that "the task of authentically
interpreting the word of God, whether written or handed on, has
been entrusted exclusively to the living teaching office of the
Church, whose authority is exercised in the name of Jesus
Christ."[31] But after this traditional statement, *Dei Verbum*
continues: "This teaching office is not above the word of God,
but serves it, teaching only what has been handed on, listening to
it devoutly, guarding it scrupulously, and explaining it faithfully
by divine commission and with the help of the Holy Spirit; it
draws from this one deposit of faith everything which it presents
for belief as divinely revealed."[32] In place of the inherited and
absolute hermeneutical priority of the teaching office over scripture, the Constitution quite unmistakably fixes a polarity between
scripture and the teaching office, since the teaching office must
answer to scripture for its decisions and base them on it.

The Twelfth Article of this same constitution draws out the
hermeneutical consequences of this polarity between scripture
and the teaching church, felt by many Catholics to be new.
Here it is stated by turns that God has spoken through men to
men in the scripture. Therefore, precise research into the original
intention of the biblical authors and writings is indispensable to
the church. In this research, exact attention must be given the
thought-, speech-, and narrative-forms prevailing at the time of
origin of the biblical writings. Only in conclusion are the single
results gleaned from this historical research to be combined with
a view to the doctrinal unity of scripture and with consideration
for "the living tradition of the whole Church . . . along with the
harmony which exists between elements of the faith." The Article continues:

> It is the task of exegetes to work according to these rules toward
> a better understanding and explanation of the meaning of sacred
> Scripture, so that through preparatory study the judgment of the

31. "Dogmatic Constitution on Divine Revelation," *The Documents Of
Vatican II*, ed. Walter M. Abbott, S. J. (New York: Herder and Herder,
1966), para. II, 10: 117–18.
32. Ibid., p. 118.

Church may mature. For all of what has been said about the way of interpreting Scripture is subject finally to the judgment of the Church, which carries out the divine commission and ministry of guarding and interpreting the word of God.[33]

The Article concludes with a passage concerning the wondrous condescension or descent of God's eternal wisdom into the word of the scripture, at which we may rejoice.

Thus today under the rubric "preparatory study" historical exegesis is integrated in the process of Catholic formation of doctrine, and in such a way that the framework in which exegesis is required to operate secures to historical criticism a merely instrumental use. Though even after the Second Vatican Council the relation between scripture interpretation and tradition and the process of official doctrinal decisions on the basis of scripture and tradition are still undefined, Catholic theology today accords itself the distinction of having "fostered the emancipation of historical-critical exegesis from 'ideological' elements and thus its technical-functional usefulness."[34]

It is already clear that the Catholic church will not be spared further hermeneutical decisions. On one side such a splendid exegete as Otto Kuss is calling the Catholic church and theology to their senses and urging the exegete to see his real task in charitably and critically confronting his church with the original witness of scripture.[35] On the other young Catholic exegetes today are quite indiscriminately appropriating all the uncertain, extravagant theses of Protestant biblical study, and are beginning such reckless experiments in exegesis that a warning is being sounded not only in their own camp but also from the Protestant side.[36] In any case the time when critical biblical interpretation was a Protestant preserve is over once and for all, and has given

---

33. Ibid., para. III, 12: 120–21.

34. Karl Lehmann, "Der hermeneutische Horizont der historisch-kritischen Exegese," *Einführung in die Methoden der biblischen Exegese*, ed. Joseph Schreiner (Würzburg: Echter Verlag, 1971), p. 63.

35. Kuss, "Exegese und Theologie des Neuen Testaments als Basis und Ärgernis jeder nachneutestamentlichen Theologie," *Schriftauslegung*, pp. 358–408.

36. See the critical symposium on the origin of the resurrection faith, with contributions by Rudolf Pesch, Walter Kasper, Karl Hermann Schelkle, Peter Stuhlmacher, and Martin Hengel, *ThQ* 153 (1973, Heft 3): 199–283, to which Hans Küng devoted a systematic postscript in *ThQ* 154 (1974): 103–17.

way to an era in which exegetes of both communions mutually counsel, criticize, and encourage each other and engage in healthy competition.

RETROSPECT AND PROSPECT

Looking back on the history of scripture exposition in the church a series of important findings emerges. Until well into the sixteenth century the church's scientific exposition found its methodological unity in allegory and its hermeneutical framework in the priority and preeminence of church and tradition over scripture. This wholistic system of interpretation collapsed when the Reformation decided upon an historically oriented theological exegesis which set scripture above the church.

In the wake of this fundamental decision Protestantism once more attempted to mesh exegesis with dogmatics so as to be independent of the fluctuations of history. But this experiment of Orthodoxy speedily failed, and since then Protestant exegesis is at pains to appropriate the method of criticism which irresistibly emerged during the seventeenth century and to practice it in the interest of evangelical faith. This pioneering decision is irrevocable and has led to an ever-increasing abundance of insights concerning the origin and uniqueness of Holy Scripture which cannot be disregarded.

Viewed from its historical roots, however, the historical-critical method implies its own system of values. Moreover its results depend most strongly on the view of history in the context of which it is used. The course of Protestant exegesis since the seventeenth century has shown that a theological use of historical method is possible only to the degree these implications of historical criticism are seen and in turn subjected to criticism. Though the extent of such criticism is still in doubt, since Schlatter, Barth, and to a degree also Bultmann it is an obvious necessity for Protestant theology, which is committed to a solely instrumental use of historical method.

Finally, the successes and experiences of Protestant critical scripture interpretation have moved Catholicism to recognize the historical criticism it had shunned for centuries as an indispensable tool of historical research, and to suit it to its own hermeneutic. To the extent this has occurred, the exegesis of both churches is beginning to reestablish contact and in part actually to overlap. It is thus this theological adaptation of historical criticism to which we owe not only all our historical knowledge of the origin and peculiarity of the Old and New Testament canon, but also the fresh encounter of Protestant and Catholic exegesis which had gone their separate ways since the sixteenth century.

Under these historical circumstances there is no occasion to speak summarily of a collapse of historical criticism. There is rather occasion to point to the gain in historical and hermeneutical insights attained by way of this method. Historical method today has an integrative capacity similar to that of allegory in the era of the ancient church.

But this vindication of the value of historical criticism may not make us unmindful of the fact that theology, for the sake of the productivity of its hermeneutic, is obliged continually to test the historical-critical method. In terms of dogmatics the perennial theological task is to consider and test the mutual relation between critical exegesis and the idea of inspiration, a relation constitutive for all hermeneutics in the area of theology. This task presents itself today not only in the Catholic sector but also and with equal urgency in the sector of Protestant theology, which from its Reformation tradition is just as clearly directed to the hermeneutical significance of the idea of inspiration as is Catholicism. The principle of inspiration points up in hermeneutical fashion that the scripture as witness to the revelation possesses an independent power and efficacy which cannot be overtaken or levelled by the most intense pursuit of a systematic exegesis, that scripture cannot be understood in isolation from the referent and experience of the church and a lived faith, and that theological interpretation can be carried on only within the horizon of a concept of truth which allows the historical contact or encounter of immanence with transcendence.

Scripture Interpretation in the Present

THE CURRENT DILEMMA

When we move from this setting of the task and from our overall historical survey to the hermeneutical problem of the present it is necessary to limit ourselves to the problems of scripture interpretation in Protestantism. Catholic exegesis is making its way on its own, and we Protestants would do well to measure ourselves by this way instead of arrogating to ourselves the role of uninvited critic. Indeed, there is ample occasion for self-criticism in Protestantism, for the reason that the multifront battle described in the Introduction is harmful to the Protestant church and theology, at present faced with fundamental hermeneutical and methodological questions which can no longer be deferred.

There are a number of reasons which compel us to speak of serious hermeneutical problems in Protestant biblical criticism. I shall refer to them from my perspective in New Testament studies.

The Collapse of Bultmann's Program

The integrative force of Bultmann's hermeneutical program is fully exhausted, chiefly for three reasons: First, the historical and biblical basis on which Bultmann founds his existential interpretation appears too narrow. In light of the comprehensive biblical canon the kerygma cannot be based merely on an existential elucidation of the Pauline and proto-Johannine preaching. Second, the role of the existential interpretation of reality and history which is constitutive for Bultmann's program and gives ontological priority to possibility over reality has spent itself historically and theologically, and the questions regarding the continuity in all of history, the laws of its succession, its meaning and teleology —questions repressed in Bultmann's day—have imperiously reap-

61

peared. Third, Bultmann's rejection of all dogmatics which gives precise content to and explains the church's confession and faith seems no longer viable, if the church is not to abandon every missionary, catechetical, and apologetic witness and explication of its faith.

If we try nonetheless to hold to Bultmann's program and establish it in the manner described as a theologically necessary and cogent hermeneutical system, in exegesis we fall prey to an explicitly dogmatic view of the text and of history, and in theology to a growing isolation from the steadily increasing problems of communication and understanding in the church today.

The Functionalism of Historical Criticism

As to the practice of historical criticism in and outside the church, since the seventeenth century a functionalism can be demonstrated which must be dealt with hermeneutically and theologically. This functionalism exhibits two major characteristics.

First, historical criticism detaches from the present the historical phenomena which it examines, and despite all tradition and the history of their effects, describes them at a historical distance. Historical criticism of the traditional variety thus distances history from the present and achieves no union of the then and the now.[1] This distancing effect is welcome and tolerable only so long as the goal of historical research is the intellectual mastery of history and the emancipation from all inhibiting tradition. But as such this cannot be the aim of a church whose very identity stands or falls by its connection with Holy Scripture.

The second characteristic of historical criticism is its functional dependence on a concept of history and reality which its practice (after the principle of analogy) assumes. If we proceed from a rationalistic notion of history and reality, the phenomena of historical tradition conformable or applicable to this concept are made to appear in markedly positive light, while conversely, all historical experiences and utterances which resist rationalism are subject to criticism or skepticism. The same reciprocal relation is repeated when we approach history with an idealistic, existential, or materialistic concept of reality and history. But if even ancient

1. On this topic, see especially the studies of Ferdinand Hahn referred to below in note 29.

history today admits it has had to learn "that the reliable ingredient in information come down to us from the past is much greater than, say, the closing nineteenth or opening twentieth century thought possible,"[2] then critical reflection on the reciprocal relation noted above is the more urgent for theology, the less frequently it can simply appropriate or sanction as theological whatever criticism or evaluation of the tradition emerges from the changing spirit of the time.

Historical Criticism and the Protestant Principle

Gerhard Ebeling, Rudolf Bultmann, and Ernst Käsemann have attempted to bring the use of historical-critical method into material connection with the Protestant principle of justification. For support they appeal among other things to the fact that an encounter with historical reality free of illusion, an encounter made possible and enforced by historical criticism, destroys all false guarantees for faith and allows man to appear once again in his sole dependence on the word. Ebeling notes in this connection:

> The *sola fide* of the Reformation doctrine of justification both contains a rejection of any existing ways of ensuring present actualization, whether ontological, sacramental, or hierarchical, and also positively includes an understanding of actualization in the sense of genuinely historic, personal encounter. If this encounter with the historic revelation takes place solely in hearing the Word, then the shattering of all historical assurances that supposedly render the decision of faith superfluous is completely in line with the struggle against the saving significance of good works or against understanding the working of the sacrament in the sense of the *opus operatum*.[3]

Bultmann expresses it still more radically when he writes in that already familiar context:

> Radical demythologization is the parallel to the Pauline-Lutheran doctrine of justification apart from works of the law by faith alone. Or rather, it is its consistent application in the sphere of

2. Hans Erich Stier, "Prämissen, Methoden und Tragweite der historischen Wissenschaft," *Moderne Exegese und historische Wissenschaft,* ed. Johannes Michael Hollenbach and Hugo Staudinger (Trier: Spee Verlag, 1972), p. 55, n. 5.

3. Gerhard Ebeling, "The Significance of the Critical Historical Method for Church and Theology in Protestantism," *Word and Faith,* trans. James W. Leitch (Philadelphia: Fortress Press, 1963), p. 56.

knowledge. Just as the doctrine of justification, it destroys all man's false security and all false longing for security, whether that security rests on his good behavior or on his validating knowledge. The man who will believe in God as his God must know he has nothing in his hand in which he might believe, that he is, as it were, up in the air, and can demand no proof for the truth of the word addressing him. For the ground and object of faith are identical. Only he finds security who lets all security go, who—to speak with Luther—is prepared to go into the inner darkness.[4]

Finally, Käsemann argues in a more dialectical fashion. First, he thetically and self-critically asserts:

Historical criticism promises and guarantees proximity to reality. That is true, of course, given the human limitation. Abstruse ideas cannot be excluded. Fantasy and caprice often throw an impenetrable net over historical reality rather than illumine it. We must devote more than half our work to refuting or correcting colleagues and unruly partisans. The old errors continually recur, and here too the waste is gigantic. History probably remains the most doubtful science. Granting all this, we will still assert and can overwhelmingly prove that we have no better means by which to get at past reality. . . . It is true indeed that the gospel establishes and mediates reality apart from and beyond all science. Still, the gospel must be critically and even historically researched if it shall remain audible, and it belongs to its authentication in daily life that it does not shut us out from the everyday character of reality, as spurious hearing and believing do.[5]

On the basis of these assertions, Käsemann establishes the theological claim of historical criticism in these terms:

Theologically, the right of historical criticism lies in its breaking through the Docetism which dominates the community. That is not its concrete task and purpose, which lies in uncovering historical reality. But that is its effect. It allows the nimbus over the biblical story to be seen as an expression of a confessing community which had to follow the call of the gospel and was thankful. It also reveals this story as a permanent conquest of unbelief in light of earthly crises and human incapacity. To that extent it demythologizes. But by so doing it willingly or unwillingly frees our gaze for the cross of Jesus, which pious ideology

4. Rudolf Bultmann, "Zum Problem der Entmythologisierung," *Kerygma und Mythos 2: Diskussionen und Stimmen zum Problem der Entmythologisierung*, ed. Hans-Werner Bartsch (Hamburg-Volksdorf: Herbert Reich, 1952), p. 207.

5. Ernst Käsemann, "Vom theologischen Recht historisch-kritischer Exegese," *ZThK* 64 (1967): 260–61.

obstructs. It sets us in the shadow of the cross as the earthly reality of salvation and offense. It is not in our power to prove God's existence and revelation. But it is our duty to display that reality in which men once came to faith. In this way we are rescued from an illusory understanding of faith.[6]

It is true that the historical method is still the best ordered means for penetrating to the historical realities, and that the declaration of justification *sola fide propter Christum* is the only true support of faith. But it is just as true that we may not screen ourselves from the negative consequences of radical Protestant Bible criticism and gild or render them innocuous by an appeal to the effects of historical criticism as serving the true faith and freeing from illusion.

In my experience the consequences are serious. For colleagues in the discipline, for pastors performing their office, and for students, historical criticism is the agent of a repeated and growing rupture of vital contact between biblical tradition and our own time. We have seen that this problem is inherent in the structure of historical criticism. As a result, a correction in respect of method is called for here.

Among the older and younger theologians at work in the church this distancing effect is accompanied by an enormous and at times even alarming uncertainty in their use of scripture. For the few who have sufficient time, energy, and schooling to occupy themselves long and intensively enough with the history of the Bible, the slogan once coined by Günter Klein, "Bible criticism as an aid to preaching,"[7] is a motto which is verified and confirmed afresh in their theological-critical exchange with the scriptural word. But for all too many who do not have this time, energy, and schooling, whose university education was too brief and irregular for them to cultivate a genuinely independent judgment on the theme and method of biblical criticism, that motto, unfortunately, does not apply. For them biblical criticism has produced a vacuum which causes them to despair of the possibilities of a useful, historical-critical interpretation of scripture, and in part to seize at hair-raising theological substitutes.

6. Ibid., p. 281.
7. Günther Klein, *Bibelkritik als Predigthilfe. Gesammelte Meditationen* (Gütersloh: Gerd Mohn, 1971).

In the dispute still crippling Protestantism today regarding the proper use of Holy Scripture, the right does not merely lie with historical biblical criticism! Rather Pietism and Fundamentalism in a manner for the most part quite inadequate theologically are reclaiming the hermeneutical necessity of the doctrine of inspiration. The longer the dispute lasts, the more the fronts will stiffen as so-called radical criticism indicates its further inability to test its Bible exposition against the claim of the doctrine of inspiration, a doctrine which is essential also to Protestant dogmatics. True, the thesis of Protestant Orthodoxy regarding the verbal inspiration of the Greek and Hebrew text is ruined beyond hope. But fitting reference to the collapse of this exaggerated view of the principle of inspiration still does not dismiss the hermeneutical relevance of the idea as a whole, the purpose of which we made clear above.

Excursus: Gerhard Maier and the "End of the Historical-Critical Method"

Theological inadequacies reflected in certain attempts to reassert the hermeneutical necessity of a doctrine of inspiration can best be illustrated by a review of the book by Gerhard Maier referred to on page 20, note 2. Maier himself once authored a significant New Testament dissertation entitled *Mensch und freier Wille nach den jüdischen Religionsparteien zwischen Ben Sira und Paulus,* (*WUNT* 12, 1971) but now asserts a priori the unreliability of historical-critical method in the exegesis of Holy Scripture:

> The concept and development of the higher-critical method present an inner impossibility to the extent that one holds to the position that the witness of divine revelation is presented in the canonical Scriptures. The method cannot prove a "canon in the canon," nor can it offer any clarity on the subject of a "divine" and a "human" Bible. In its concentration on subject matter, it is not able to grasp the person-structure of the Bible. The method cannot do without preconceived ideas of what "genuine faith" or "the Word of God" is. Because its results are lacking in practicability, this method is unsuitable or at least inadequate in the eyes of the church. But the most important objection is that historical criticism over against a possible divine revelation presents an inconclusive and false counterpart which basically maintains human arbitrariness and its standards in opposition to the

demands of revelation. Therefore because this method is not suited to the subject, in fact even opposes its obvious tendency, we must reject it (p. 25).

Maier would rather retreat behind the historical-scientific ranking of the biblical books with other ancient sources (made since Semler) and behind the distinction between the scriptural text and the word of God (in use since Semler) to an evaluation of the biblical canon as the inerrant source of revelation and the inspired word of God.

Maier's great model is thus Lutheran Orthodoxy's doctrine of scripture and its inspiration (see pp. 59–80). On behalf of this rehabilitated, fundamentalistic view of the canon Maier even censures Luther's critical utterances on the canon for their subjectivity. Though at the conclusion of his book Maier himself arrives at the judgment that we can designate Christ "the middle of Scripture and its pivotal point, its center, its heart" (p. 92), he allows Luther's well-known verdict from his Preface to James and Jude of 1522 and 1530 to stand—"the true test by which to judge [that is, according to the usage of that period: to test critically] all biblical books" is to see "whether or not they teach Christ [*Christum treiben*]"—but only as an inherently precarious point of contact for that modern Protestant theology which historically or systematically has set about the hybrid attempt to detail such an intra-biblical canon.

Maier regards all such recent attempts on the part of Willi Marxsen, Herbert Braun, Werner Georg Kümmel, Ernst Käsemann, Hermann Diem, Gerhard Ebeling, Wilfried Joest, and others as having failed. In critical debate with Käsemann, he even ventures such a statement: "Whoever makes justification of the ungodly his focal point on which all theology should be based, and stamps just this as the 'specifically Christian,' banishes important lines and basic thoughts of Scripture into powerless darkness" (p. 40). Together with the Catholic Hans Küng, Maier declares Protestant concern for exegetical inquiry into the midpoint of scripture as an ultimately subjectivistic and arbitrary attempt "to be more Biblical than the Bible, more New Testamently than the New Testament, more evangelical than the Gospel, and even more Pauline than Paul" (p. 45, with a quote from what Maier calls Küng's "brilliant critique" of Käsemann). In reviewing the allegedly vain attempts of Protestants to arrive at a canon in the canon, Maier himself regards it as settled "that Scripture itself does not offer a canon in the canon, but . . . the latter is exacted forcibly and against its will" (p. 49).

Maier continues:

> What kind of a horrible providence would it be for God to allow us to search for a binding canon so long and so despairingly with only the result of increasing uncertainty! The constant witness of Scripture confirms that certainty is the goal of God's love and the

content of the prayer: "Order my steps in Thy Word, and let not any iniquity have dominion over me" (Psalm 119:133), while uncertainty originates out of opposition to God. If there should really be a canon in the canon, then not only would Scripture have to be divorced from the Word of God, but also Christ from the Scriptures, the Holy Ghost from the Scriptures, and the one Christ of Scripture from the other Christ of Scripture. The light of a new Docetism would then fall on the event of the Incarnation and on certain parts of Scripture. The canon in the canon would move into dangerous proximity to being a mere idea; the contingency of history would, to say the least, be attacked. For the impartial hearer of the Word, those would obviously be nonsensical results (p. 49).

After this fulminating denial of the whole scientific-theological implementation of the Protestant principle of justification in the last two to three hundred years, Maier sets himself and others the task of developing

> an exegetical method of exegesis which is in accord with revelation in the form of the Holy Scriptures. This includes surmounting the philosophically based cleavage between Scripture and the Word of God introduced by Semler and his colleagues. This implies nothing less than vanquishing English Deism, French skepticism, and the German Enlightenment in the domain of theology (p. 50).

The true slogan should read: "A historical method? Yes! A critical method? No! or Caution!" (p. 50); and the thesis of the program is: ". . . the historical-critical method is to be replaced by a historical-Biblical one" (p. 52). For this method, the following rules apply: (1) "Suspending the compelling principle of analogy," and with that, insistence upon a "basic difference between general historiographic methodology and theological methodology" (p. 51). (2) Regard for the "sovereignty of God" in the revelatory event, that is, the correlation of "revelation and obedience, not revelation and critique" as an epistemological rule. "Thus it has been stated correctly: *credo ut intellegam* (I believe in order to understand), not *credo quia intellego* (I believe because I understand). Therefore it must be clear to us that right doctrine presumes right living, also on the part of the individual theologian. Without being born again, we remain as ignorant as Nicodemus" (p. 54). (3) Regard for the congregation's spiritual experience of scripture, that is, of the spiritual unity and activity of Holy Scripture, borne out in the life of the congregation.

In practice, for Maier the historical-biblical method should then be oriented to what is useful in earlier historical criticism, but include only the following steps: First, what Maier calls "finding the text," in which a "comparison of variants must be carried out critically" [!], not in terms of an arbitrary text criticism, of course, and yet "with reasonable and intelligent standards" (p. 80). Second, a translation solidly founded in philology and the history of language. Third, a thorough "illuminating" of the "contemporary historical background" (p. 82). Fourth, a historicoreligious comparison, which must be aware of the "divine revelation exclusively within Scripture" (p. 83). Fifth, since "in the area of literary criticism and form criticism . . . we will note a vast difference between a historical-Biblical methodology and the historical-critical" (p. 83), a literary or formal investigation—"in order to avoid erroneous results" (p. 84)—should wherever possible be coupled with the historicoreligious comparison and the comparison with contemporary history. Only in his investigation of hymns, prayers, and parables may the expositor more closely pursue the redactional stages of a text. Sixth, the biblical utterances should be subjected to a "Biblical classification," that is, ranged within the "various *epochs* in the history of God's dealings with man [*Heilsgeschichte*]" (p. 84), as well as within the dynamic structure of the scriptural utterances as a whole. Seventh and finally, the exegete should strive for a "balanced analysis, faithful to the context" (p. 86), which has as its goal "a total view of what has been gained from the previous procedural steps, and . . . logically culminates in one or more sentences that summarize the primary content and scope of the text" (p. 86). Maier adds: "An analysis becomes theological only when the interpreter gives expression to *what God here wants to say to all men*" (p. 87, italics in Maier).

Maier's sketch and his book as a whole are satisfactory neither in details nor in basic features. We might set it down to one of those common criticisms of Ernst Käsemann to which pietists feel obliged when Maier burdens himself and his readers with the patently grotesque misjudgment that in his interpretation of justification Käsemann, of all people, fails to emphasize and value "God's creating and renewing activity" (p. 40). But the errors go deeper.

In the first place, the way in which Maier describes for himself and his readers the hermeneutical problem of scripture exposition in the church is quite inadequate. He articulates neither the problem and risk in the exegesis of the ancient church and the Middle Ages, nor the magnitude of the Reformation's new hermeneutical departure within the limits of an ecclesiastical system of exposition. The reader learns nothing at all of the differences between Luther's and Calvin's view of the problem of inspiration, or of the distinction between scripture and preached word of God, a distinction which does not at all originate with Semler, but with the Reformation. He learns nothing of Orthodoxy's ahistorical abridgement of the Reformation attempt, or of the reasons why Pietism and Free Thought once made common cause against Orthodoxy. The book virtually conceals the true history of the problem of Protestant hermeneutics since the Enlightenment. It does not touch on or evaluate the new turn in the hermeneutical debate in our century.

Second, with a single stroke of the pen Maier surrenders the church's claim to a scientific basis for its biblical exegesis, a claim made since Origen's time and in our century renewed by Bultmann and Schlatter alike. In its place he sets once more the requirement of a spiritual, self-evident Bible exposition within the circle of the reborn, a requirement which came to grief a hundred times in church history from Christian Gnosticism to every shade of fanaticism.

Third, the dogmatic basis for Maier's spiritual hermeneutic as well as for his historical-biblical method—in which even allegorical elements are not to be totally rejected (p. 74)—is quite inadequate. In my opinion Maier represents an unfortunate meld of Reformation hermeneutics, deprived of theological rigor and freedom, with that Catholic doctrine of interpretation restated in the *Dei Verbum* of Vatican II, a meld in which the infallibility of the teaching office is replaced with the inerrancy of the biblical canon. But the question as to how and by whom Christ is to be recognized as the midpoint of scripture is left open when Maier alleges that exegesis can arrive at such a midpoint only in an improper and arbitrary way, but at the same time rejects any claim to infallibility on the part of a teaching office in the church.

Since Maier thus omits to furnish his readers any information on the dogmatic basis for his new idea—in addition to what we have just noted the book lacks cogent arguments for establishing and confirming the church's confession from the scripture and does not really penetrate to the dogmatic problem inherent in a spiritual exposition— no answer is given as to how the group which agrees to this new method of interpretation can actually secure its faith against its own miscalculations. But in a Reformation church it is precisely this question which may not remain open.

Finally, we must state that Maier's half-hearted dependence on historical criticism will bring the expositors he leads into the greatest difficulties, particularly in their exegetical practice and apprehension of truth. There is little consistency in warning against authentic text criticism and in the same breath requiring a critical sifting of the textual variants; in harboring suspicion against literary- and form-criticism and then allowing them in the investigation of hymns and parables; in paying homage to the old scopus method which constricts the texts and then, by citing the angels' desire to pry in 1 Peter 1:2 (p. 84), expressly enjoining the exegete against probing the biblical process of redaction and proclamation, though still charging him with a universal, theological exposition of texts. How shall the interpreter speak intelligently and intelligibly of his texts when rational insight into the origin of their proclamation is denied him beforehand? Maier's directives are thus quite impractical from the standpoint of method, and as for the kerygma, they tempt to merely biblicistic protestations and repetitions.

After all this, we must give the author back his book with a plea for drastic revision. Württemberg Pietism is served only when we do not fall behind Adolf Schlatter in the matter of method and content.

A Synopsis of Results

What has just been said can be illustrated and carried forward when we are forced to give a synopsis of the extravagant experimental results in current radical New Testament criticism. In doing so we learn with what vast proof of performance historical criticism today confronts theological students, the church, and the public concerned for the Christian faith.

While one group of researchers turns the so-called historical Jesus, uncovered by historical research back of the Gospels, into what Heinrich Schlier sarcastically termed "a fifth Gospel and the test of the other four" (in part, even of the entire New Testament),[8] others contend that the quest of the historical Jesus is not only theologically incorrect and useless, but is today incapable of historical solution, since the texts dealing with Jesus in the Gospels are almost totally overlaid and in a majority of instances even manufactured by the faith of the post-Easter Christian community.

Since the reports in Acts concerning the founding of the primitive community in Jerusalem are judged far and wide to be purely legendary, and since the question as to the sources edited by Luke is for the time being mired in indecision, there is a gap in time between the record of Jesus in the Gospels and the preaching of Paul. The gap can only be filled with such sparse texts from the tradition as 1 Corinthians 15:3–5 or Romans 3:25–26, but there is absolutely no agreement on the contexts and locales in which those texts were transmitted. Thus in the opinion of some scholars we can only hint or guess at the preaching of the primitive community and those first impulses toward Christian Jewish and Gentile mission.

As for Paul, historians regard him as representing Hellenistic

8. Heinrich Schlier, *Das Ende der Zeit, Gesammelte Aufsätze 3* (Freiburg: Herder, 1971), Introduction p. 11.

missionary Christianity, quite distinct from the primitive community. His epistles, inclusive of Romans, are subjected to the most reckless theses in regard to redaction and interpolation. Theologically, Paul is viewed as the apostle of a doctrine of justification which declares forgiveness only to the individual and which sets the individual's eschatological existence solely on that faith which hears the message of God's saving deed in Christ and acknowledges it as applying to itself. The same research which draws this esoteric portrait of Paul also and to a degree even passionately spurns the attempt to indicate more precisely the christological basis for justification in Paul. It even regards the statement of Jesus' atoning death as a questionable tradition which Paul already got the better of theologically and to which he referred only in quotations. This research speaks only in loose fashion of the "cross-event" which establishes justification, or perhaps of the vicarious obedience of Jesus who goes to his cross, an obedience which (but how?) frees us. Some elevate this vaguely founded proclamation of justification to a canon within the canon and from it evaluate and critique the proclamation of Christ in Colossians, Ephesians, Hebrews, the Pastorals, the Catholic epistles, in Revelation, and also in the Synoptics. Others attest that Paul, precisely on account of this proclamation and the apocalyptic expectation which he joined to it, was surprisingly limited by the situation, and accordingly declare him to be as hostile to the world and change as the historical Jesus.

In the letters of Paul's pupils the dynamic of the Pauline train of thought is already arrested, and early Christianity, in the view of many, is being exposed to a speculative, Hellenistic Christology which the epistle writers can only contain with great effort. In the end, however, this domesticated Christology paves the way for a disastrous, early Catholic absolutizing of the church.

Among the Synoptists Mark, in pioneering the earliest plan for a Gospel, is said to be at pains to establish a synthesis between two complexes of tradition. The first (mis)represents Jesus after the Hellenistic model as a divine man and thaumaturge. The second, in the form of a passion narrative allegedly pieced together from many single traditions at a very late date, gives scarcely adequate information about the true setting of Jesus' crucifixion. It is stated that Mark's plan was originally designed for a Jesus-sect located in Galilee. With this comprehensive account Mark meant to win this sect for the true Christian kerygma of Jesus' cross and raising by attempting to lead it from mere adherence to Jesus to a true faith in the kerygma. Mark's Gospel is thus an evangelistic Jesus-narrative, calculated to lead away from mere faith in Jesus.

It is alleged that the material of the Sayings-Source, edited by Matthew and Luke in addition to Mark's Gospel, originally belonged to a peculiar Syrian Christianity which chose to know nothing of the saving significance of Jesus' death and raising. Accordingly, the redactional assimilation of this material into the synoptic framework with its passion and atonement Christology is said to suit the church's earliest domestication of an old, radical Syrian Jesus-theology.

The Gospel of John, not referred to till now, and in its allegedly original form still free of ecclesiastical embellishment, critical of the sacraments and eschatology, appears to some as the second great pillar of the New Testament kerygma alongside Paul. But others claim that it is the document of a Christian Gnosis, adopted only belatedly and at great pains through churchly redaction, and fitted into the canon only under cover of the early-Catholic epistles of John. By appeal to the man Jesus, begotten of Mary and Joseph (see John 6:42), this Gnosis originally taught a this-worldly retreat from the world, and to that end made use of mythological interpretative devices.

Finally Luke, hard pressed by circumstances of the time and by anxiety for the church's continuance, is said on that account to have surrendered the Pauline gospel of Christ to a salvation-historical scheme which anyone can verify. The scheme begins with the Old Testament promise, has its normative midpoint in the time of Jesus, and ends with the time of the church, a time to be concluded by the (remote) last day.

Since the historical reliability of Acts must be seriously questioned, according to recent opinion a history of primitive Christianity, if at all, can only be written in rough outline and with considerable gaps. But in light of the fragmentary traditional material the attempt to compose a theology of the New Testament meets with almost insuperable difficulties and must in any case surrender the traditional notion that the New Testament contains a variety of theologically supportable and convincing lines of unity.

Finally, the biblical canon—narrowly viewed as embracing only the New Testament—is supposed to have been created by the ancient church from out of an anti-heretical instinct for self-preservation. It is binding upon theology today only insofar as it exhibits a theologically acceptable center. One is advised to refer back of the canon and the entire New Testament literature to the historical Jesus as the criterion of all New Testament tradition and contemporary faith. But with this recourse to Jesus, the series of contradictory theses and hypotheses begins anew.

Admittedly, this synopsis is one-sidedly oriented to the extravagantly critical theses now being discussed, and to that extent is tendential and also "elenctic," that is, prepared toward the need for rebuttal. But of late, and since the appearance of Joachim Kahl's *The Misery of Christianity*,[9] and Rudolf Augstein's *Jesus, Son of Man*,[10] we cannot deny such synopses are in fact being privately or even publicly produced, since the publications containing these extravagant theses are accessible to all. But if they are being produced and if our survey offers just one possible summary of current historical-critical analysis of the New Testament, then we have rightly estimated the uncertainty and skepticism which this work arouses.

In light of our sketch one of two conclusions can easily be drawn. One can agree with Otto Kuss on the agony of a Protestant biblical criticism free of all dogmatic restraint and insist that in view of such vast uncertainty of judgment only the teaching, inspired church can guarantee the saving necessity of a distinct, biblically founded proclamation of faith, and thus that the Catholic route is the only viable route in hermeneutics.[11] Or one can turn to disciplines which for Protestant theology appear more productive than the problem-area of New Testament

9. Joachim Kahl, *The Misery of Christianity*, trans. N. D. Smith (Harmondsworth: Penguin Books, 1971).
10. Rudolf Augstein, *Jesus, Son of Man* (New York: Urizen Books, 1977).
11. Otto Kuss, "Über die Klarheit der Schrift," *Schriftauslegung*, pp. 143–49. See also pp. 392–400 from the essay by Kuss, cited on p. 58, n. 35.

exegesis, which has made of the biblical canon such a ruinous heap of hypothetical possibilities.

Political Theology

When we take fully into account the fact that in the vacuum and exegetical uncertainty in which we find ourselves we are actually being summoned to recall the original, emancipating, and enlightening power of historical-critical method, and in the theological ferment after the death of God to turn to a political hermeneutic and theology, we must definitely pay heed. This political theology intends to orient itself to the humane and social-critical impulses which remain to us from the biblical literature. It emphasizes that "from a Christian point of view, theory and praxis can be understood today only in their unity, which means truth is not something that we find or by which we are found, but something that we make true."[12] Political theology holds that the biblical proposition "that God loves all of us and each and every individual" is "a universal theological truth which without translation becomes the universal lie," and that the "translation" of this proposition needed today is "world-transforming praxis."[13] However simplistic and ontologically deficient the notion of truth propagated here, the summons of political theology more easily finds listeners the less sure theology and the church are of their political ethics, and the more anemic the material resistance which the biblical disciplines can give that notion turns out to be.

12. Dorothee Soelle, *Political Theology*, trans. John Shelley (Philadelphia: Fortress Press, 1974), p. 70. I am not certain, of course, whether Soelle intends to stand by these simplistic theses. In an essay dedicated to the relation between religion and experience entitled "Die Reise zum vergessenen Ganzen," *Ev Komm* 7 (1974): 543–45, she reproaches the Marxist criticism of religion for "a (self)estranged reduction of human reality" (p. 544), urges respect for the human religious need, and writes: "In a variation on a theme of Freud, 'Where It was, I shall be,' we can say: 'Where the alien, the accidental, and the nothing were, shall be home, identity, and God.' The word 'God' then no longer denotes a superior force at home in another world and which penetrates our world from the outside. It no longer denotes another sphere, heaven, another time after death, another kind of immortal, almighty Essence encountering us as person. But we do need the word 'God,' in order to express the totality of our world not yet attained, the truth of our life not yet manifest" (p. 545). Apart from the ever burning question whether such a version of the concept of God still makes Christian theology possible, it would be interesting to see how Soelle intends to define the relation between that truth which "we make true" and the "truth of our life not yet manifest."
13. Soelle, *Political Theology*, p. 107.

A WAY OUT OF THE DILEMMA

If we intend to take none of these paths which lead us away from exegesis, then we must ask in all seriousness whether or not our historical, New Testament exegesis requires a fundamental reconsideration of its course and its methods. That is, if we were left with the historically fragmented and in part even absurd survey sketched above, in my judgment it would mark the end of the labor of a theological discipline which has abolished its relevance by its critical work. Such an abdication would have painful results for the Protestant church which in essence appeals to scripture.

But we are not yet to this point. There is still a possibility for self-criticism and reform. The strength of the critical biblical sciences has always been their capacity for self-correction. Till now they have never neglected in time to rectify their gross and obvious errors. We have reason to hope for this now in the historical and biblical-theological work of friends and many colleagues; a labor for the most part quiet, always selfless, and rarely appearing in the glaring spotlight of an ecclesiastical public grown hungry for sensation. This work proves that a biblical-scientific study of the Old and New Testament, consistently but not artificially pursued, and based on a solid knowledge of the sources, gives the lie to that ruinous panorama of results—and that also means to the method leading to these results when perennially used in one-sided fashion. It thus provides a heartening basis for further work.

If in awareness of this fact we attempt a way out of our dilemma, we must realize that the problems besetting us emerged throughout a long history. Not merely the efforts of many, but great patience and certainly considerable time is needed to arrive at a new and truly convincing solution. At the moment, only a few proposals for improvement can be submitted which require critical discussion and testing.

The Connection with Dogmatics

In my opinion, a way out would be found if Protestant exegesis were again to strive for contact and connection with a dogmatics able to correct and guide it, above all a dogmatics which not merely exhausts its strength in theological-historical analyses, but moves on toward its own affirmations and judgments. Protestant exegesis by nature has an intimate relation with systematic theology and lacks direction and orientation to the degree that it seeks to loosen or even surrender this relation. Historical exegesis should thus be aware of its dissimilarity to dogmatics, which is charged with a contemporary account of the faith. It should realize that it is dependent on such a dogmatics and can neither shunt nor monopolize the dogmatic tasks. Exegesis requires an orientation session with a dogmatics conscious of the tradition and the present. Among other things, the history of hermeneutics teaches that this session must return to the questions of scripture inspiration and the hermeneutical significance of the Third Article, since exegesis is continually in danger of forgetting how and at what place it must be theologically active.

When we inquire more precisely as to what kind of help dogmatics gives to exegesis in its current insecurity, we must note two things. We must first see how each dogmatics views theology as a whole, and second, what direction biblical exegesis receives from this total picture.

JÜNGEL

Eberhard Jüngel defines Protestant theology as "a science which in all its parts is related to the event of God's word and constituted solely by this relation."[14] Authentic and timely proclamation of the word of God takes place beyond theology as science, namely "in the praxis given by the Holy Spirit."[15] According to Jüngel, theology as science is related to this praxis in the church but is not to be equated with it. In the area of scientific theology the task of the exegesis of Old and New Testaments is to trace the "word event which *takes its origin* under the historical conditions of this world."[16] It carries on this work

14. Eberhard Jüngel, "Das Verhältnis der theologischen Disziplinen untereinander," *Unterwegs zur Sache, Gesammelte Aufsätze* (Munich: Chr. Kaiser Verlag, 1972), p. 54.
15. Ibid., p. 56.
16. Ibid., p. 58, italics in Jüngel.

by critically interpreting the texts available to it in reference to Jesus Christ as the word of God in person.[17] It does so by the aid of a method which satisfies the claims of historical science, but which is tested by dogmatics in historical theology to determine that it does not atheistically rule out God.[18] As a historical discipline exegesis of the Old and New Testament is also a theological discipline and must retain this identity under the guidance of dogmatics straight through to its consciousness of method. Unfortunately Jüngel does not yet give precise information as to what effect this has or must have in respect of method. He merely states the thesis that "the tension between historical and dogmatic understanding is to be eased by a critique of historical reason which is still in the offing."[19] From Jüngel, then, we get only a bearing for our own further work.

MILDENBERGER

In his *Theorie der Theologie* Friedrich Mildenberger moves more directly toward the matter of our concern. His basic conception of theology agrees with that of Jüngel. For him as well

17. With this requirement, Jüngel (p. 58, italics in Jüngel) draws a very precise distinction between Old and New Testament study in the following four theses: (1) "Old Testament study relieves the other theological disciplines by *keeping silent* about Jesus Christ." (2) "New Testament study relieves the other theological disciplines by allowing the biblical texts as a whole to speak of Jesus Christ. Without New Testament study, Old Testament study would cease to be a theological discipline." (3) "In particular, New Testament study relieves Old Testament study from special historical responsibility regarding the *end* of the Old Testament." (4) "In particular, Old Testament study relieves New Testament study from special historical responsibility for the theological presupposition of the gospel." Though Jüngel does not construe the mutual "relief" of the disciplines as a limiting of horizons but only as concentration within the awareness of a problem common to all, in my opinion we must ask whether or not these theses might hinder interaction in biblical exegesis, and in some instances give systematic legitimacy to the unsatisfactory status quo of the work in both disciplines— contrary to Jüngel's intention. On this question, see also Wolfhart Pannenberg, *Wissenschaftstheorie und Theologie* (Frankfurt a. M.: Suhrkamp, 1973), p. 353.

18. In Jüngel's own words: "Historical theology explains its objects, and thus God's word, by reckoning with the world *etsi deus non daretur* (as if there were no God). Dogmatics 'in' historical theology, however, must account for what is to be historically explained in such historic fashion that it does not allow historical theology to reckon with God *etsi deus non daretur*. To the extent dogmatics does this it accounts for the historical method in theology in a truly authentic way and preserves theology as a whole from becoming either schizophrenic or atheistic" (p. 52).

19. Eberhard Jüngel, "Die Freiheit der Theologie," *ThSt* 88 (1967): 31.

theology is the science of the word of God. As "instruction in the art of church government"[20] it is not to be directly identified with the word of God which takes shape in the church's mediation of the saving work of Jesus Christ to an evil world,[21] but it is constitutive for the church and its witness of faith. Thus for Mildenberger also the word of God is christologically defined. What makes his theses so important for us is that he turns more directly than Jüngel to the problem of method in theology, and thus discusses the biblical-exegetical task.

According to Mildenberger, biblical exegesis—for pragmatic reasons divided into the Old and New Testament disciplines, but from the viewpoint of the canon to be seen as a unity—has the task of uncovering the original witness of the Old and New Testaments for use in the church. In order to do this in a scientifically and theologically responsible manner, biblical scholarship, as other theological disciplines, must pass through two stages of reflection, a historical-critical stage and a dogmatic-normative stage. In the historical-critical stage the original meaning of the texts is researched with the usual historical tools. In the dogmatic-normative stage its applicability for the church is probed. Both processes are indispensable, but they are to be kept distinct.[22]

When we ask how the texts are to be applied we arrive at the dimension of a spiritual understanding of scripture in the sense

20. Friedrich Mildenberger, *Theorie der Theologie* (Munich: Chr. Kaiser Verlag, 1972), p. 15. The formulation is oriented to Schleiermacher's definition of Christian theology in paragraph 5 of the *Brief Outline on the Study of Theology*. There Schleiermacher writes: "Christian theology . . . is that assemblage of scientific knowledge and practical instruction without the possession and application of which a united leadership of the Christian Church, i.e., a government of the church in the fullest sense, is not possible." Friedrich Scheiermacher, *Brief Outline on the Study of Theology*, trans. Terrence N. Tice (Richmond: John Knox Press, 1966), p. 20.

21. Mildenberger's formulation, p. 20.

22. In Mildenberger's own words: "We should . . . respect the uniqueness of the historical-critical method and not burden it with the problematic of application—with which, *nota bene*, not merely theological, but also general hermeneutics must struggle (see Hans Georg Gadamer, *Truth and Method*, translation by Garrett Borden and John Cummings [New York: Seabury Press 1975])," Mildenberger, *Theorie der Theologie*, p. 84. His advice is worth considering, but it cannot and may not mean that historical study dare be relieved of its awareness of the methodological problem, an awareness reached by Gadamer and further developed by, for example, Hans Krämer (see note 28 below).

of the church's tradition. Mildenberger himself emphasizes this and tries to indicate, in a way which today is feasible but which is also rooted in the Reformation, how such spiritual exposition might look. His answer is as follows:

Spiritual interpretation in the church was never a mere private reading of scripture for edification during prayer and meditation, but always an exposition which led to common statements of faith. These statements exist in the shape of old and new confessions recognized in the church. Lifted out from scripture and summarizing its essential content of faith, these confessions in turn must lead to a better understanding of scripture. This too is in accord with Reformation tradition. Spiritual exposition would thus mean to reenter this circle of understanding which encompasses critical exposition and confessional tradition (as a guide to understanding in interpretation) and to demonstrate "that the intent of the biblical texts is disclosed to such an understanding—and only to such!—which allows itself to be led by the witness of those who heard the scripture before us."[23] Mildenberger is aware that his suggestion is opposed by modern Protestantism's innate reaction to the phenomenon of confessions and their hermeneutical function. But he still hopes for the one who will risk reentry into a circle of understanding already proved in the Reformation, hopes for "an exegesis . . . which does not attack the texts with the customary hermeneutical acts of violence, but allows them finally to state their case."[24]

Altogether, Mildenberger's advice is to advance from an historical-critical procedure to a dogmatic-normative exegesis, by which this "spiritual" exposition focuses on the question to what degree the confessions received in the church are confirmed by the literal sense of scripture, and vice versa. In this way, Jüngel's directional clue is given precision by Mildenberger, through an outline of theological exposition reminiscent of Barth's hermeneutical model. Indeed, both Jüngel and Mildenberger counsel against simply distancing ourselves from the scientific consensus

23. Mildenberger, *Theorie der Theologie*, p. 94.
24. Ibid.

of our time by replacing historical method in the biblical disciplines with another type or with a type of historical exposition suited to the aims of theology.

PANNENBERG

In his impressive programmatic sketch, *Wissenschaftstheorie und Theologie,* Wolfhart Pannenberg's discussion of biblical exegesis aims precisely at this requirement. In contrast to Jüngel and Mildenberger, Pannenberg would prefer to loose theology from its functional dependence on the empirical church and reestablish its scientific character by conceiving it as a theology of religion per se. The object of this theology of religion is God, the all-determining reality, or more precisely, historical reality as a whole in which God indirectly manifests himself as the reality which destines everything for his future. Christian theology is only a species of the universal theology of religion because and while it devotes itself to the nature and truth of Christianity, a phenomenon still to run its course. Christianity of course lives from the faith that God, the all-determining reality, has appeared in Jesus Christ with such finality that since Jesus' raising from the dead all history is clearly a process of confirming and verifying this faith, and will have its consummation in Christ's return.[25] But till the end of history when God is directly manifest, this faith is in dispute. Put scientifically, in every age it must maintain its hypothetical claim to truth against those religions which proceed from another historical and final manifestation of God. The real ontological presupposition in Pannen-

---

25. In Pannenberg's own words: "The *uniqueness* of Christianity . . . can be properly described only as that process of historical consequences which resulted from and are repeatedly kindled by the basic tension in Jesus' preaching of the Kingdom of God. Christianity is not, e.g., the result of this process which made its entry at some point in the primitive Christian period; and it is not identical with Jesus' message which forms its starting point. Rather, it is in essence this process itself, which lives from out of the basic tension in Jesus' message and its absolute consolidation in the event of his cross and resurrection. An 'Essence of Christianity' cannot be loosed from this process, the dynamic of which is at work to the present day. . . . The essence of Christianity is itself this history between the advent of God's future in the appearance of Jesus, and the future of God's Kingdom under the sign of the returning Christ." Pannenberg, *Wissenschaftstheorie und Theologie,* p. 420, italics in Pannenberg.

berg's concept of theology is the continual openness and inevitability of the religious question regarding God as the all-determining reality. The theological question which is appropriate to this concept, decisive for it, and which unites all the disciplines taking a hand in this theology, is the question as to how God has appeared in history and to what sort of religious mastery of reality this appearance led in traditional times, can lead today, and will lead in future.

Within this total scheme of a Christian theology rooted in the history of religions—a scheme which Pannenberg has constructed by consciously resorting to basic ideas in theological liberalism and historicism—falls the task of biblical studies. For Pannenberg also, Old and New Testament exegesis can be separated pragmatically, but not programmatically. They share the task of describing the decisive beginnings in the Jewish-Christian formation of tradition, that is, "the task of a coherent description of the history of tradition in Israel and primitive Christianity, in which political-institutional history and a description of the views of faith are integrated."[26] Analysis of individual biblical texts and attention to the problem of the canon are only a part of this integration of religious-historical and theological tasks. Accordingly the still dominant historical-critical method can only help us enter upon the task but not discharge it in a truly satisfactory way.

In order to be productive within the framework of a theology of religion the method needs broadening in at least two respects. First, it must be able to allow room for the question of God and his activity. Second, it must have an eye for the phenomenon and significance of comprehensive historical processes which are still open in respect of their future, that is, for processes which are never simply to be set down as "profane" but always as successions of events in which the fundamental religious question of God is put and decided.[27] In order to be theologically productive, historical criticism requires transformation after the

26. Ibid., p. 392.
27. Pannenberg gives this problematic special treatment in the context of his definition of church history as "the history of the religion of Christianity." Ibid., p. 395; see also pp. 398–99.

measure of a comprehensive-historical, religiously structured understanding of reality.

Hence for Pannenberg theological interpretation is first of all an exegesis which advances beyond the historical analysis of facts and texts to the question as to how the biblical texts have conceived the self-disclosure of God, the all-determining reality, in history, what this idea has achieved toward the mastery of reality in the biblical period, and to what degree this biblical concept of faith can be normative for later epochs of Christianity. On this last question concerning the contemporary relevance of biblical religion, biblical exegesis can and must allow itself to be "relieved" (to use Jüngel's term) by church history, systematic theology, and practical theology.

Thus in contrast to Jüngel and Mildenberger Pannenberg urges a programmatic broadening not merely of the area of exegetical activity but also of the traditional historical method, so that it may be a useful tool for religious-historical work. We must take this demand to heart—methodologically Pannenberg himself does not carry it out in detail—to the degree we recognize the dilemma of present-day New Testament criticism. But we can do so only to the extent that historical theology, by establishing a method of its own, does not forfeit its claim to scientific prudence and verifiability. In other words, we agree with Pannenberg only to the degree that theology, in its scientific-historical work and in the method which shapes it, can succeed in the ontological battle for the religious dimension of reality. Aided and instructed in our task by this survey, we move to a second proposal.

The Hermeneutics of Consent

Exegesis would find a way out of its dilemma if it could resolve to test its methodological and hermeneutical tools along with their praxis currently in vogue. It should thus be our goal to fashion a *Hermeneutics of Consent* to the biblical texts which is reasoned out both as to method and the history of effects.

According to what we learned in the discussion with dogmatics, this catchword cannot denote a special theological hermeneutic.

Its aim is rather to indicate what is at issue today in dealing with ancient texts,[28] among which the biblical traditions enjoy special rank only for Christianity. The interpretation of these biblical texts is a test-case, a special instance of historical criticism as such, and biblical exegesis has no leave rashly to break out of the theoretical consensus in the historical sciences.

OPENNESS TO TRANSCENDENCE

In a hermeneutics of consent we need first to recall that as early as the nineteenth century the attempt at an objective, naturalistic view of history was defeated.[29] Then, to the degree it is ontologically possible, we need to lay hold of the insight of the "new hermeneutic"—the studies of Hans Georg Gadamer, Ernst Fuchs, and Gerhard Ebeling—into the lingual dimensions of historical reality. Third and finally, we need to consider how complex the existence of the world and man is for us today.

These insights can help relax that insolent attitude of control which in the intellectual and technical area threatens to alienate our entire human existence and renders every claim on the individual—from the tradition, from the present and the environment, or even from transcendence—an imposition or restriction on his right to freedom which he must resist. It appears to me that one of the essential anthropological and ontological questions of our time is whether we will succeed in getting free of this absolutist stance toward emancipation and find our way to a new openness

28. In this connection, I refer with particular pleasure to the essay of my Tübingen colleague Hans Krämer, "Zur Ortsbestimmung der historischen Wissenschaften," *Zeitschrift für allgemeine Wissenschaftstheorie* 5 (1974): 74–93, which in the formulation of the question and the problem partly parallels my own reflections.

29. In an essay entitled "Probleme historischer Kritik," which on the whole is important and worth noting, Ferdinand Hahn writes: "It is precisely in light of the biblical tradition that we should be able to recognize the markedly defective view of history which has stamped historical criticism and to great degree still determines it. As long as inadequate and even inhibiting premises are not conquered here, we cannot get free of the difficulties in contemporary exegesis." ZNW 63 (1972): 17. On the problem see also Hahn's review of the state of the discipline in "Die neutestamentliche Wissenschaft" in *Wissenschaftliche Theologie im Überblick*," ed. by Wenzel Lohff and Ferdinand Hahn (Göttingen: Vandenhoeck & Ruprecht, 1974), pp. 28–38; and the study by Walter Wink, *The Bible in Human Transformation* (Philadelphia: Fortress Press, 1973), with its energetic, one-sided, but in substance often telling criticism of the still dominant tendency in contemporary historical biblical criticism to objectify and isolate.

to the world, that is, a willingness to open ourselves anew to the claim of tradition, of the present, and of transcendence.[30]

For hermeneutics and for dealing with our texts, this means that we may not use the traditional historical method merely to inquire in critically one-sided fashion how *we* relate to the texts and how the texts, gotten at through the principles of analogy and correlation, can be ranked in an ancient context of events. This line of inquiry obviously retains its full right. But in addition we must again learn to ask what claim or truth about man, his world, and transcendence we hear from these texts. If we explicitly include this principle of hearing in our historical work, a principle for a long time implicitly recognized and observed by respectable historical and religious-scientific study, then historical criticism will initiate a "critical dialogue with the tradition."[31]

This dialogue is important, since in dealing with an historical tradition we must always realize how much we live from and by it. This is true especially, but by no means exclusively, of the biblical tradition. Just as all tradition, so the biblical tradition supports, empowers, and limits our life at one and the same time.

The hermeneutics of consent does not spell a flight from this comprehensive context, but a consciousness of it and a consent to the existence of a textual and spiritual tradition which makes its claim on us in the twofold sense indicated above. Only from a conscious affirmation of our tie with tradition are we enabled or even forced to engage in an active dialogue with the current tradition regarding its durability or need for transforming.

METHODOLOGICAL VERIFIABILITY

Today, the second requirement of a hermeneutics of consent

---

30. Most instructive in this connection is Gerhard Ebeling's debate with the *Traktat über kritische Vernunft* by Hans Albert, 2te Auflage (Tübingen: J. C. B. Mohr, 1969), which appears in "Kritischer Rationalismus?" Beiheft 3 to *ZThK* 70 (1973).

31. The late Leonhard Goppelt, who in his final studies repeatedly agreed with my analysis of the problem in *ZThK*, 68 (1971): 121–61, under the title "Neues Testament und Hermeneutik—Versuch einer Bestandsaufnahme," chose this very slogan to describe the heremeneutical task of New Testament exegesis. See his "Prinzipien neutestamentlicher und systematischer Sozialethik heute," *Die Verantwortung der Kirche in der Gesellschaft*, ed. Jörg Baur, Leonhard Goppelt, and Georg Kretschmar (Stuttgart: Calwer Verlag, 1973), p. 8; and his *Theologie des Neuen Testaments* 1, ed. by Jürgen Roloff (Göttingen: Vandenhoeck & Ruprecht, 1975), p. 41.

is that altogether and in its detailed use it must as far as possible be verifiable as to method, reasoned out, and capable of correction. I give this such special emphasis because I have in mind the strange refusal of an entire group of New Testament colleagues seriously to come to terms with the problem of method in historical study. There are four reasons why the problem of methodological structure in biblical exegesis must be taken seriously.

First, in what preceded we continually came up against the functionalism and autonomy of historical method. This must be dealt with if it is not always automatically to drive us into a rut. Second, we must demand of exegesis that its treatment of texts be scientifically verifiable, and that means capable of scrutiny as to method. Otherwise, historical interpretation of scripture would become an intuitive vision, limited to an individual or group, scarcely or no longer communicable. Third, exegesis should be reasoned out in respect to method, since only by scientific and theoretical apprehension of the way in which we handle the tradition can we master the continually astonishing and at times even horrifying experience that a historical exposition of texts seldom leads to really commonly recognized results, but as a rule yields quite disparate data. The reason for this is that historical study always contains an element of subjectivity and that the complex combination of methods which comprises history study (text- and literary-criticism, form- and redaction-criticism, lexicography and the history of religions) can be quite variously used and accented.

There is a fourth reason for requiring verifiability in method. It lies in the fact that only when we see clearly what our historical methods can and cannot do are we really able to measure to what degree we actually need additional psychological and sociological, even linguistic categories and methods of interpretation to broaden and give precision to our understanding of tradition. Of late, we are confronted with ever new attempts at regaining a multidimensional exposition of scripture.[32]

32. The essay by Walter Wink, *The Bible in Human Transformation* (Philadelphia: Fortress Press, 1973), gives a particularly interesting example. A New Testament scholar at Union Theological Seminary in New York, Wink wants to get free of a historical criticism preoccupied with distancing and

We can render a reasoned judgment on the productivity of such proposals for correction only when we ourselves are ready to enter the debate concerning method.

Our requirement that hermeneutics be scientifically verifiable and reasoned out in respect to method in no way contradicts that attitude of consent or principle of hearing to which we referred. On the contrary, it actually appears that this scientific anamnesis of humane and religious features in the tradition is a way especially suited to the mentality of the modern man, by which to rediscover and recapture dimensions of existence which have been forgotten and believed to be lost.

EFFECTIVE-HISTORICAL CONSCIOUSNESS

Finally, we must require of a hermeneutics of consent that it reflect on its own locale of interpretation as well as on the fact that a history of effects and of interpretation lies between us and the texts to be interpreted. This is a history we cannot simply ignore, because it has something essential to say to us about the way we interpret as well as about the impulses given off by the texts. It ultimately determines our interest or disinterest in the historical tradition. In interpreting such tradition this history must thus be observed, and its chief data perceived and as a whole carefully used.[33] The tradition from which we come as biblical exegetes was in part already familiar with this hermeneutical principle, so that what is needed in regard to this third requirement is merely the conscious revival of an earlier used and theologically tested mode of interpretation.

objectifying texts by channeling the practice of biblical criticism and providing it feedback through a wholistic experiential and interpretative model of biblical, New Testament texts. This method has been tested for three decades by Elizabeth Boyden Howes and the Guild for Psychological Studies in San Francisco, California. A German translation of Wink's work appeared in 1976: *Bibelauslegung als Interaktion* (Stuttgart: W. Kohlhammer, 1976), and contains an instructive postscript by G. M. Martin. I am sure Wink's book will enrich the current discussion of the possibilities and limits of a psychological interpretation of biblical texts.

33. As examples of such exegesis, see the study by Martin Hengel, *Christ and Power* (trans., Everett R. Kalin; Philadelphia: Fortress Press, 1977; original German edition 1974), and my commentary, *Der Brief an Philemon: Evangelisch-Katholischer Kommentar zum Neuen Testament* (Neukirchen: Neukirchener Verlag), 1975. Hengel has given his exegesis a theoretical base in a series of theses, "Historische Methoden und theologische Auslegung des Neuen Testaments," *KuD* 19 (1973), 85-90.

THE REFORMATION MODEL

We have just outlined a hermeneutics of consent which should qualify us for enriching dialogue with the historical tradition and its truth. Now we must specifically ask what this type of interpretation, which not merely critically dissects but also listens, can accomplish theologically. When we consider the history of interpretation in the church and in Protestanism, the answer seems to me to be clear: By the hermeneutics of consent, done in our own contemporary and scientifically studied fashion, we re-establish connection with the Reformation's hermeneutical model of Bible exposition.

Protestant Orthodoxy had restricted this model in such a manner that it no longer left room for a free and historical formulation of the question. Protestant exegesis had thus first to free itself from the Procrustean bed of an orthodox, ahistorical, theological treatment of the Bible. It had to achieve an unrestricted view of the original shape of the Old and New Testaments and establish possibilities for a historical-critical exegesis of the Bible. But once Protestant exegesis has established these possibilities and with that perceived what historical method can and cannot do, it can and must recall that exegesis which serves the church must be hermeneutically equipped to deal with the self-sufficiency of the scriptural word, the horizon of the Christian community's faith and experience, and the truth of God encountering us from out of transcendence.

If we test our hermeneutical model to see whether it is elastic enough to do justice to these hermeneutical claims raised by the ancient church and the Reformation, we come, in my judgment, to a positive result. When we consciously begin from the basic principle of consent and of hearing, we remain open to the church's experience that the biblical texts disclose a truth which wakens faith and does not lie within the scope of human possibility. We can, of course, prepare for and disclose an understanding of this truth by a thorough historical interpretation of scripture, but its ultimate effect upon our wills lies with that truth and not with us. In a hermeneutics of consent, therefore, there is room for the self-sufficiency of the scriptural word.

The same is true of the horizon of the church's faith and

experience. If, according to Paul and the Gospel of John, the Holy Spirit is active as the power of faith and a true understanding of Jesus, and if without him there can be neither faith nor an understanding of Jesus as Revealer and Reconciler (1 Corinthians 12:3; Galatians 3:2; John 14:24–25, 16:12–13), then for hermeneutics this means that the biblical texts can be fully interpreted only from a dialogical situation defined by the venture of Christian existence as it is lived in the church. We do justice to this second hermeneutical requirement of a theological exegesis of Holy Scripture when we invite to genuine dialogue with the tradition of the text and to an awareness of the history of the text's interpretation and effects which determines it.

Finally, this also applies to the third hermeneutical dimension of theological exegesis—openness to an encounter with the truth of God coming to us from out of transcendence. We have expressly demanded of a hermeneutics of consent that it be open to the language of transcendence. Whoever refuses this openness—for example, through an existential decision on behalf of the sole validity of the critical, left-wing Hegelian model of theory and praxis, for which truth appears merely as a human possibility—can interpret the historical tradition only in a very fragmentary way, and the biblical tradition in a way no longer appropriate. He must either totally reject the biblical propositions which speak of God's truth, or alter them to historical and anthropological statements. In this connection it is still true that we cannot establish by a method the recognition of the biblical proclamation of the truth, at the center of which Jesus is the embodiment of a love which reconciles and conquers even death. But we can say and we can see that the hermeneutical principle underlying the interpretation of biblical texts must be an openness to the possibility of faith. The hermeneutics of consent satisfies also this last requirement.

This hermeneutic and the historical interpretation of the text which follows it can be effected in one of two ways. First, in the attitude of *fides quaerens intellectum*, that is, as a Christian believer and member of the church who intends to renew and clarify for himself and others the Christian confession of faith out of a dialogue with scripture. Second, in the attitude of *intellectus quaerens fidem*, that is, as advocate of a listening intellect who is open to the Christian tradition and the possibility of address through the biblical kerygma, without himself being able to rise to faith in the truth of this message.

Thus our hermeneutical model is not and cannot intend to be a special theological model, because God and the Holy Spirit cannot be confined to a method. But we can still speak of a similarity and even of a certain hermeneutical congruence between our model of interpretation and that of the Reformation, as well as of those traditions of exposition in the ancient church on which the Reformation hermeneutic rests. What we have achieved beyond the ancient church and Reformation is the possibility and freedom of making use of historical criticism where it is really productive, namely in historical analysis and description, and at the same time of transcending it where it threatens to restrict our encounter with historical reality.

SUMMARY AND PROPOSAL

The total result of our inquiry is as follows: Historical-critical exegesis is not in and of itself theological interpretation of scripture. But it can be such when it is hermeneutically reasoned out as an interpretation of consent to the biblical texts, and when it is carried on theologically in regard for the enduring hermeneutical relevance of the Third Article of the Apostles' Creed.

Since methodological considerations alone cannot aid a discipline, it may be permitted a New Testament scholar to conclude with a concrete exegetical and theological proposal. It is historically imperative that we resist the hypothetical unravelling of the New Testament tradition into a multiplicity of single strands, solitary communities, and isolated theologies which can no longer be correlated. With good reason and the prospect of success, we can attempt the outline of a synthetic biblical theology of the New Testament which is consonant with developments in the history of Israel's language[34] and religion,

34. On the phenomenon and problem of a history of the biblical language, see Klaus Koch, *The Growth of the Biblical Tradition: The Form-Critical Method*, trans. S. M. Cupitt (London: A. and C. Black Ltd., 1969), pp. 106ff.

and which extends to the formation of the Christian canon. This theology can and must be open to the Old Testament as the principal basis for the formation of the New Testament tradition, while the proclamation of Jesus Christ as the Messianic Reconciler is its genuinely theological and critical center.[35]

35. See my essay, "Das Bekenntnis zur Auferweckung Jesu von den Toten und die Biblische Theologie," *ZThK* 70 (1973): 365–403, and my three studies which extend the substance of this essay: "Jesus als Versöhner," *Jesus Christus in Historie und Theologie.* Festschrift für Hans Conzelmann zum 60. Geburtstag, ed. Georg Strecker (Tübingen: J. C. B. Mohr, 1975), pp. 87–104; "Zur Neueren Exegese von Römer 3:24–26," *Jesus und Paulus.* Festschrift für Werner Georg Kümmel zum 70. Geburtstag, ed. Earle E. Ellis (Göttingen: Vandenhoeck & Ruprecht, 1975), pp. 315–33; and "Zur paulinischen Christologie," which will appear in coming essays in honor of Nils A. Dahl.

Indexes

BIBLICAL REFERENCES

AUTHORS